Johnson's Island

CIVIL WAR IN THE NORTH

Johnson's Island

A Prison for Confederate Officers

Roger Pickenpaugh

The Kent State University Press · *Kent, Ohio*

© 2016 by The Kent State University Press, Kent, Ohio 44242
Library of Congress Catalog Card Number 2015036106
ISBN 978-1-60635-284-7
Manufactured in the United States of America

Quotations from the J. L. Stockdale Diary, from the Confederate Prisoners of War Collection in the Alabama Department of Archives and History, appear courtesy of the Alabama Department of Archives and History. Quotations from the Papers of Thomas Gibbes Morgan Sr. and Thomas Gibbes Morgan Jr. appear courtesy of the David M. Rubenstein Rare Book & Manuscript Library, Duke University. Quotations from the John Harvey Reece Civil War Diary, 1864–1865 (part of the John H. Reece Civil War Papers, AC 1990–0011M) appear courtesy of the Georgia Archives. Quotations from the Robert Bingham Papers, Joseph Mason Kern Papers, Luther Rice Mills Reminiscences, and Virgil S. Murphey Diary appear courtesy of the Southern Historical Collection, Wilson Library, The University of North Carolina at Chapel Hill.

Library of Congress Cataloging-in-Publication Data
Pickenpaugh, Roger, author.
  Johnson's Island : a prison for Confederate officers / Roger Pickenpaugh.
    pages cm. — (Civil War in the North)
  Includes bibliographical references and index.
  ISBN 978-1-60635-284-7 (pbk. : alk. paper) ∞
1. Johnson Island Prison. 2. United States—History—Civil War, 1861–1865—Prisoners and prisons. 3. Ohio—History—Civil War, 1861–1865—Prisoners and prisons. 4. Prisoners of war—Ohio—Johnson Island—History—19th century. I. Title.
  E616.J7P53 2016
  973.7′71—dc23
                        2015036106

20 19 18 17 16   5 4 3 2 1

To

ANYA and MIKE

with wishes for happiness

Contents

Acknowledgments

As with so many other books, the greatest debt incurred in writing this one is to my wife, Marion. As in the past, she assisted in the research process, helped compile the index, and listened patiently to my ideas and complaints.

My mother, Fern Pickenpaugh, was again an eager proofreader.

Family in northern Virginia made research trips to the National Archives and the Library of Congress much easier and much more fun. Thanks to stepdaughters Anya Crum and Jocelyn Brooks, Anya's boyfriend, Mike Huie, and Jocelyn's husband, Patrick, as well as grandchildren Parker and Harrison Brooks.

Locally, members of the Noble County (Ohio) Authors' Guild, including Wes Bishop, Tammy Kirchner, Jim Leeper, Mary Lou Podlasiak, Gary Williams, and Ken Williams, provided both assistance and sympathetic ears. Jim also spent hours guiding me through those aspects that required computer skills.

Archivists at the institutions listed in the bibliography were universally professional and personable. So was the staff of the Sandusky Public Library, where I secured photos. I remain indebted to the staff of the Muskigum University Library in New Concord, Ohio. They handled a large number of interlibrary loan requests, saving travel time and expense. Thank you, Zelda Patterson, Nicole Robinson, Jamie Berilla, and Elaine Funk.

This is my first adventure with the Kent State University Press. I hope it will not be the last. They have been courteous, professional, and understanding of inane questions and my near total lack of computer skills.

1

"Decidedly the Best Location"

Establishing the Prison

Montgomery Meigs was a realist. He had to be. As quartermaster general of the Union Army, he was also a man charged with tremendous responsibilities. A career officer, fifth in the 1836 graduating class at West Point, Meigs had gone on to a solid career as an engineer in the peacetime army of the 1840s and 1850s. His crowning achievement—in a near-literal sense—was the dome of the United States Capitol, which was nearly completed when the guns aimed at Fort Sumter fired on April 12, 1861, plunging the nation into civil war. The following month Meigs was promoted to brigadier general and named to the post that he would hold during the four years of the war. His daunting task was to keep the Union armies supplied and on the move. In doing so, Meigs would eventually oversee spending in excess of $1.5 billion.[1]

Unlike many of his civilian superiors, General Meigs realized that the war was likely to be long and difficult, and he urged officials to plan accordingly. On July 12, writing to Secretary of War Simon Cameron, he addressed an issue that other officials had overlooked. "As in the conflict now commenced it is to be expected that the United States will have to take care of large numbers of prisoners of war," Meigs wrote, "I respectfully call your attention to the propriety of making some arrangements in time." The quartermaster general called for the appointment of a commissary general of prisoners. This official would be "charged with the care of prisoners now in our hands and preparations for those likely to fall into our possession." Meigs also urged that a site be selected for "a depot and place of confinement for prisoners of war." Specifically, he recommended "the Put-in-Bay Islands of Lake Erie."[2]

Cameron approved the recommendations, and Meigs issued orders to put them into effect. In early October he named Lt. Col. William Hoffman to the post of commissary general of prisoners. The son of a career army officer, Hoffman had followed in his father's footsteps. After being graduated from West Point in 1829, he served at a succession of frontier posts. During his three decades of service, he had established a reputation as a strict and capable officer. "Although never brilliant," his biographer notes, "he was an able and efficient officer." He was also notoriously thrifty, insisting that buildings be constructed of the cheapest materials and that his men provision themselves by raising their own crops. At the posts he commanded, Hoffman established a "post fund" by reselling surplus rations to the commissary. The fund was used to purchase such luxuries as an ice house, a bowling alley, and curtains for post buildings.[3]

His prewar duties, including the erection of Fort Bridger and the rebuilding of Fort Laramie, provided Hoffman with practical experience that would serve him well as he oversaw construction of the Union's proposed prison. He also brought brief experience as a military prisoner to his new position. Hoffman had commanded the 8th United States Infantry, stationed in Texas, when that state seceded. His superior officer, Gen. David Twiggs, surrendered the unit to a state home guard and promptly joined the Confederate Army. Hoffman and his men were quickly paroled, and they started north after pledging not to take up arms or serve in the field against the Government of the Confederate States of America until exchanged. This made Hoffman available for the post of commissary general of prisoners. He did not want the job, lobbying for a special exchange that would free him for duty in the field. His efforts failed, and good soldier that he was, Hoffman assumed his new duties. Except for a few months in late 1864 and early 1865, he would remain in the thankless position for the remainder of the war.

On October 7, 1861, Hoffman headed for Lake Erie to select a suitable site for what was then expected to be the Union's sole military prison. He first inspected North, Middle, and South Bass Islands on the American side of the lake. All three posed problems. Both North Bass and Middle Bass, he felt, were too close to Canadian islands, raising the dangers of escape or rescue. South Bass was largely occupied by vineyards, posing a strong temptation to the men who would garrison the post. In addition, all three islands were too far from Sandusky, the nearest city, to transport construction materials efficiently. Hoffman next visited nearby Kelley's Island. He found it to be a likely site except for the presence of a "wine and brandy establishment." The commissary general feared the business would pose "too great a temptation to the guard to be overcome by any sense of right or fear of punishment."

"I examined also an island in Sandusky Bay opposite the city," Hoffman then reported. It consisted of about three hundred acres and was located two and three-quarter miles from Sandusky. Some forty acres of land were cleared, "affording a good site for the buildings fronting on the water toward the city." There was much to recommend the site for the budget-conscious officer. The entire island could be leased for just five hundred dollars a year. There was also a large amount of fallen timber, which could be utilized as fuel. Because of the island's proximity to Sandusky, large storehouses would be unnecessary at the post. Hoffman concluded, "I recommend this island—Johnson's Island—as decidedly the best location for a depot I have seen."[4]

The commissary general suggested the erection of "a substantial plank fence to inclose [sic] the ground on three sides [and] a high open picketing closing the fourth toward the water for security in winter time." He believed a gate and a large blockhouse should be placed at one of the interior angles and recommended a smaller blockhouse at the angle nearest to the lake. "A hospital, storehouses and kitchen will be required," Hoffman noted, "and probably mess-rooms as there will be scant room for eating in the quarters." All of this, plus barracks for prisoners and guards, stoves, fencing, and outhouses, Hoffman estimated would cost $26,266.[5]

On October 26 Meigs approved Hoffman's plans and ordered him to proceed at once to Sandusky. "In all that is done," the quartermaster general urged, "the strictest economy consistent with security and proper welfare of the prisoners must be observed." This stricture was in line with Hoffman's views. Still, the commissary general showed a willingness to spend money when he believed such expenditures were necessary for "the proper welfare of the prisoners." When he sent Meigs a copy of the lease on November 15, Hoffman informed his superior that he had allowed the contractors an extra allowance of $1,500 to make sure the buildings would be suitable for the winter climate. He also reported, "Much of the lumber is already on the ground and the work is progressing rapidly." The contractors, Gregg & West of Sandusky, he considered "energetic, reliable men."[6]

Writing about these events thirty years later, one of those energetic contractors, W. T. West, recalled that Hoffman had at first desired a location closer to Detroit. The commissary general's mother and brother lived in the Michigan city, and he felt that it would be a cheaper market for lumber. "I did not suppose that we should stand any chance," West wrote. He tried to improve his hometown's chances by securing lumber at a bargain price and submitting a bid to Hoffman that trimmed twenty-five percent from the estimated construction price. Despite these efforts, West was surprised when he received a telegram from Hoffman informing him that Johnson's Island had been selected.

The construction of a major military depot proved an economic boon for Sandusky. In addition to the construction and lumber contracts, the city's merchants were called upon for a variety of needed supplies. On December 7 the *Sandusky Register* reported that local businessman A. H. Gale had been awarded a $1,500 contract for supplying stoves. The contract called for 170 heating stoves and 20 of "Peckham's Improved Agricultural Furnaces and Boilers." Hoffman urged commanders at all Union prisons to utilize these large-capacity cooking boilers, which saved money because they required a minimum of fuel.[7]

A warm autumn allowed the contractors to push the work forward rapidly. On January 27, 1862, Hoffman informed Meigs that all the buildings had been completed. All that remained was for the contractors to finish the bunks and benches in the prison barracks. The commissary general had hoped that carpenters among the guard company then training on the island would do this work and also construct the fence. He could not find any, however, and was forced to give these extra tasks to the contractors. This added to the final cost. So too did Hoffman's decision to increase the height of the fence from nine to eleven feet. The cost conscious Meigs trusted his equally frugal subordinate. He approved all of the Johnson's Island expenditures.[8]

Meigs could certainly not have objected to Hoffman's thoroughness. The summer and fall of 1861 saw few Union victories. Few victories meant few prisoners, and the commissary general was able to devote his full energies to the construction of the Johnson's Island depot. As the buildings went up he issued orders that the stables be built near the water and far enough from the main camp to avoid any danger from fires. On November 10, 1861, he asked the commander of the Allegheny Arsenal in Pittsburgh for advice about casemate carriages for the twelve-pound howitzers he wanted for the two blockhouses. Later he arranged with the same officer for ordnance and ordnance stores. In February Hoffman made arrangements with the state of Ohio's quartermaster department to provide blankets. Meigs agreed to supply surplus clothing for the prisoners. Hoffman felt that this would be needed, "as it will be desirable to throw away many of the filthy garments which the prisoners will have on when they arrive here."[9]

On January 3 Hoffman sought permission to purchase a small steamboat for the prison. Meigs may have questioned the necessity for such a vessel, because on February 5 Hoffman wrote, "After maturely considering the matter of a guard boat for the Depot, I cannot advise the substitution of a launch or row boat in place of a steam propeller." The steamboat was necessary, he explained, to prevent possible attacks and to discourage escapes. Also, smaller vessels would become unmanageable "during the prevalence of heavy winds, which are common in the spring and fall." The quartermaster general was persuaded and instructed Hoffman to locate a guard boat for the post. Perhaps the search was unsuccessful. In any event Johnson's Island did not get its boat until July.[10]

One of Hoffman's greatest challenges came in attempting to find a commander for his Lake Erie prison. As the commissary general of prisoners would soon discover as he attempted to staff a number of Union prisons, the best men had volunteered their services at the front. His options limited, on December 28 Hoffman selected William Seward Pierson as commander of Johnson's Island with the rank of major. Contractor West later claimed that it was his influence that secured the position for the thirty-seven-year-old Sandusky mayor. "He knew nothing about military tactics," West conceded, "but was a clever fellow." The commissary general appeared to agree with that assessment. In seeking the approval of Ohio governor William Dennison for the appointment, Hoffman admitted that the new commandant had "no experience in military matters." However, "from the high regard entertained of him by gentlemen in whom I have great confidence as a gentleman of the strictest integrity, an intelligent and experienced man of business, particular in administrative affairs, and from my own observation of his gentlemanly and courteous manners I feel well assured that he will fill the station in a way to meet the best interests of the service and the satisfaction of those under his charge."[11]

Hoffman was even more open with Dennison's successor, David Tod. Writing to the new governor in April 1862, he expressed regret that a more experienced officer had recently refused command of Johnson's Island.

William Seward Pierson, a former mayor of Sandusky, was Johnson's Island's first, and longest serving, commander. (Courtesy Massachusetts MOLLUS Collection, United States Army Military History Institute, Carlisle Barracks, Pa.)

Pierson, he noted, was "very gentlemanly and courteous" and "very industrious and attentive." However, "the commander must have some military experience, the more the better, and he should be a little advanced in life, as years will give weight to his authority." Hoffman added, "He [Pierson] appreciates his deficiencies and is very willing to resign his place into more able hands if such are within my reach." They were not, and Pierson would remain in command at Johnson's Island until January 1864.[12]

With no replacement in sight, Hoffman did all he could to advise his young commander of military protocol. His often prickly disposition had earned him the nickname "Old Huffy," but Hoffman couched his instructions to Pierson in terms that were almost fatherly. He urged his newly minted major to avoid consulting members of his command before issuing orders. "The more silent the commanding officer is about his measures the better the effect," Hoffman counseled. He further instructed Pierson not to overlook details. "The neglect of trifles leads to other neglects, and step by step discipline is undermined," he wrote. Finally, Hoffman called for strictness. When he sent the commander instructions in relation to drill, he noted that the duty might seem "pretty hard" to some. "There may be complaints against it even by officers," Hoffman warned, "but if soldiers are required to do only what they are willing to do there can be little discipline or instructions."[13]

Hoffman also anticipated difficulties in finding a competent surgeon for the prison. Under regulations the pay would be only eighty dollars per month. The physician would also have to live on the island. Under those circumstances, Hoffman explained to the surgeon general, "I doubt if any competent person can be found to accept the place." The surgeon general granted permission to raise the pay to one hundred dollars a month, and on February 15 Pierson informed Hoffman that Dr. Timothy Woodbridge had accepted the appointment. "I send a telegram to you requesting you to employ him immediately," the relieved commissary general replied.[14]

To secure a guard force for the prison, Secretary Cameron turned to Governor Dennison. On October 29, 1861, the war secretary asked the governor to raise "a select company of volunteers" for the duty. Dennison replied that he would "cheerfully comply" with the request and would consult with Hoffman in the selection of officers. Hoffman informed officials in Washington on December 28 that the first twenty-five men had reported to the island. By then two companies had been recruited. Ten days later Hoffman sent word to Ohio's adjutant general that the first company, commanded by Capt. Foster Follett, was "about organized." He asked the state official to supply arms and equipment, including a revolver for each man.[15]

At Dennison's suggestion the outfit was christened the "Hoffman Battalion." Later it would be brought up to regimental strength as the 128th Ohio Volunteer Infantry, but for the time being the challenge was getting enough men to fill the ranks of the outfit. On New Year's Day, 1862, the following recruiting ad appeared in the *Sandusky Register*:

HOFFMAN BATTALION!

$100 Reward

Men enlisted to garrison Government station on Johnson's Island, receive the above Bounty in addition to good pay, excellent quarters and abundant rations.

Men must be of good height, and between the ages of twenty and forty. ONE HUNDRED MEN WANTED IMMEDIATELY.

They will receive the same military instruction that enlisted men do in the regular service, and draw the same pay.

Pay and subsistence begin from the date of enlistment.

N. B.—Non-commissioned Officers of this Battalion will be filled from the ranks, and every man enlisting will be eligible to the appointment.

B. W. WELLS

Lieut. Hoffman Battalion[16]

As the buildings went up and the Hoffman Battalion trained, Sandusky residents received little information about what was going on such a short distance away. Accounts of activities on Johnson's Island were rare in the *Register,* which proved to be one of the advantages of locating the post on an island. Still, the occasional discouraging word did leak out. One anonymous Sandusky resident complained in early March 1862 that Mayor Pierson had not yet resigned his political office. On January 21 the *Register* reported that a bridge constructed between the city and the island had been found to be "sadly defective" and unsafe. The project is something of a mystery. The paper did not mention whether local or federal officials were responsible for the construction of the bridge. The work is not mentioned in surviving Johnson's Island records.[17]

The most serious charge came from John Carr, a Sandusky contractor, who complained to Meigs that fraud had played a part in the awarding of the construction contract. After receiving Carr's March 18 letter, Meigs asked Hoffman for his views on the matter. The commissary general explained that the approaching winter weather had compelled him to award the contract quickly. Gregg & West, he added, had come highly recommended. "I was not disappointed in the men," Hoffman concluded. Meigs passed the explanation along to Carr, and there the matter apparently rested.[18]

These problems aside, work on the island continued at an impressive pace. On February 24 Hoffman had informed Meigs that the prison was ready to receive five or six hundred prisoners. Although the physical facility was largely completed, Hoffman still harbored concerns relating to security. He did not feel the guard force was sufficiently trained to take charge of large numbers of prisoners. In addition, the revolvers he had requested had not yet arrived; nor had the lanterns he had ordered for nighttime security. Sandusky Bay was also not ready to cooperate. The winter's ice was breaking, making a crossing to the island quite dangerous.[19]

These matters paled in comparison to a new challenge Hoffman was about to receive. Eight days before he sent his message to Meigs, Gen. Ulysses S. Grant had demanded the unconditional surrender of Fort Donelson. When the Tennessee fortification capitulated, the Northern people had a new hero and the Northern Army had an open path via the Cumberland River to Nashville. The Union also had fifteen thousand prisoners and a major logistical problem on its hands. Wiring his superiors, Grant conceded, "It is a much less job to take them than to keep them." He suggested a policy of paroling all prisoners taken in future battles, an idea he would later come to reject. As Grant began to forward his captives to St. Louis, he noted, "I fear they will prove an elephant."[20]

Grant's capture rendered Hoffman's prison on Lake Erie woefully inadequate. He had designed it to house 1,280 prisoners, fewer than ten percent of the number of Rebels the Union now had on its hands. As the commissary general saw to the finishing touches at Johnson's Island, other officers made arrangements to house Grant's captives. Foremost among them was Gen. Henry W. Halleck, who, as commander of the Department of the West, was Grant's immediate superior. A desk operator, known as "Old Brains," Halleck found the prisoner situation a challenge he was well suited to handle. Some prisoners ended up at a former medical college in St. Louis. Others went to the abandoned state penitentiary at Alton, Illinois. Most were transferred to one of four posts that had been established as Union training camps: Camp Douglas at Chicago; Camp Butler near Springfield, Illinois; Camp Morton, on the Indiana State Fairgrounds near Indianapolis; and Camp Chase, located four miles west of Columbus. Some would eventually make their way to Johnson's Island, but Union officials were about to determine that the population of the Sandusky depot would be limited to the elite of the Confederacy.[21]

2

"A Prison for Officers Alone"
Early Days of Operation

As General Halleck forwarded General Grant's captives to a variety of midwestern camps, Hoffman watched helplessly. The prison he had devoted four months to building still could not accommodate any of them. Sandusky Bay remained the problem. "I returned [to Sandusky] from Columbus last evening," he wrote Meigs on March 2, "in the hope that I would be able to make arrangements for the immediate reception of some of the prisoners, but the ice is still in too uncertain a condition to permit me to advise that any be sent here at this time." It was not until the thirteenth that he was able to report that the bay was clear and prisoners could finally be sent to Johnson's Island. By then the commissary general knew from where he wanted the first group sent. He had recently returned from an inspection tour of the facilities that had been pressed into service as military prisons. Among the worst he had seen was a "pork house" at Lafayette, Indiana, staffed by a surgeon he considered incompetent. Hoffman requested that the prisoners there be among the first sent to Sandusky.[1]

It is not certain when the initial contingent of Confederate captives reached Sandusky, but it was likely the two hundred Rebels who arrived at the railroad depot on the evening of April 10. They were definitely the first group to attract the attention of Sandusky citizens. Just two weeks earlier Governor Tod had asked Halleck to transfer two hundred fifty officers then held at Camp Chase to the Lake Erie facility. The governor followed up with an impassioned plea. "It is very important that at least two hundred . . . of the most dangerous should be transferred to Johnson's Island or elsewhere," he wrote Halleck on April 8. Halleck relented, apparently without consulting Hoffman, and instructed Tod to transfer "such of the prisoners of war as you may deem proper."[2]

The *Register* had a reporter on hand for the arrival. He noted that the prisoners were sent from Camp Chase, and he offered the following description of the Rebels:

> They were clad variously. Some had on the characteristic butternut colored [*sic*], and some did not. Some wore blue coats with brass buttons; others had on coats of no particular color, and as for buttons, we saw none. Some wore hats and some had on caps—none were bareheaded save when they raised their head-coverings. . . .
>
> Some of them had something of the bearing and carriage of gentlemen and some had a different carriage. Some had the don't-care-a-dime swagger of bloods, some were sullen in appearance, while others seemed to forget themselves in their curiosity to see the sights. . . .
>
> An average of their features would be marked with a case-hardened sort of an expression, shaded with a malicious frown. We suppose they represent the flower of the chivalry of the South. If there was anything about them superior to the "greasy mechanics" of the North, which they affect to despise, we could not see it.[3]

Three days after this batch of Confederates reached Lake Erie, Secretary of War Edwin M. Stanton, who had succeeded Cameron, sent the following message to Hoffman: "You will cause the officers, prisoners of war, at Columbus to be removed without delay to the Sandusky depot, which will hereafter be held as a prison for officers alone." No explanation was given for this special status. It is likely that the added security offered by the island location was foremost in Stanton's mind. Hoffman carried out the order, asking Governor Tod to send the officer prisoners north from Columbus in increments of two hundred. He informed the governor that new quarters were going up at Johnson's Island but the capacity was still limited. The commissary general warned that, in the meantime, Camp Chase might have to serve as a temporary holding facility for officers.[4]

Hoffman had made plans for the new barracks, which he called "blocks" at Johnson's Island, in March. On the 17th he submitted a proposal to Meigs for the project. Gregg & West again received the construction contract. The plan called for the erection of two-story blocks for the prisoners and a hospital with a capacity of 170. Meigs gave his approval, adding, "As you are the commissary-general of prisoners you best know what is necessary." What was necessary eventually grew to some one hundred structures. By the end of 1863 Johnson's Island had thirteen prisoner blocks, ranging from 117 to 130 feet long. Twelve of them rested on two parallel rows of six. One row contained the even numbered blocks, the other the odd numbered blocks. Block 13 sat between and parallel to Block 11 and Block 12.[5]

Among the prisoners arriving at Johnson's Island during the spring of 1862 was Capt. John Henry Guy of the Goochland Light Artillery. Although raised in Virginia, Guy's four-gun battery ended up at Fort Donelson, where it was surrendered with the remainder of the garrison. Guy first went to Camp Chase, arriving on March 1, then was part of a group of officers that was transferred to Johnson's Island on April 24. After five days at the prison, Guy compared the two facilities. On the negative side, the Johnson's Island sutler was both difficult to track down and had a more limited stock of goods, and he also charged higher prices. "But when we consider the increased extent & the beauty of our prison grounds," Guy explained, "the improved water, the fine breezes, the fine prospect around us, & the healthiness of this place, we are satisfied with the change."

At times it seemed that Guy was describing a vacation resort rather than a military prison. "The enclosure is about 250 yards wide and 300 yards long," he wrote, "containing about 15 acres & affording the amplest room for exercise & for active sport with ball. The ground is very level & beautifully turfed." Guy's main complaint stemmed from the fact that he had not been among the very first prisoners to arrive. Those in the initial contingents had occupied the best blocks, leaving Guy and his comrades in "undesirable buildings." However, even in this area Guy was charitable. "But as matters are all in confusion yet, we hope to fall upon an arrangement which may better our condition."[6]

Guy was one of many diarists who passed through the gates of Johnson's Island. As a prison set aside exclusively for officers, the depot housed a large number of literate—even loquacious—captives. Among them was Capt. Andrew Jackson Campbell of the 48th Tennessee Infantry. Like Guy, Campbell was captured at Fort Donelson, and he too arrived at Camp Chase on March 1. Two months later he was transferred to Johnson's Island. According to Campbell, the railroad trip to Sandusky from Columbus was a pleasant one. "We got plenty of the ardent aboard at Columbus by bribing a sentinel with a bottle of whisky," he wrote. "The boys all kept very lively and made some bold remarks to the women and men collected at Shelby to see the living Rebels." At Sandusky they were met by a Union captain who had been "shot to pieces" in western Virginia. The veteran soldier treated the prisoners kindly. "His plan," Campbell recorded, "was to meet together, take a big drink and settle the war."[7]

Like Guy, Campbell was pleased with the location of the camp, but he also had reservations. "Although this prison is situated in a splendid place and where the winds off the lake constantly fan it," he wrote, "yet it is infested with vermin and creepers on the ground and back of the kitchen." Although he observed on May 19 that it was cold enough for overcoats, Campbell later noted, "Prisons in warmer climates certainly are much worse and filthy in the extreme." As he never had to endure a Lake Erie winter, that observation was never put to the test.[8]

As the spring wore on, officers from other Union prisons were transferred to Johnson's Island. On June 21 Hoffman ordered those at Camp Douglas to Sandusky. The day before, a contingent had arrived from Governor's Island, located below the tip of Manhattan where the East River empties into New York's Upper Bay. Included in the group was Capt. William Henry Asbury Speer of the 28th North Carolina Infantry. Speer had been one of 730 Confederates captured at Hanover Court House, Virginia, on May 27. As would so many of his comrades, Speer commented upon the kindness of the line soldiers who guarded him before he arrived at the prison camp. One took his canteen and filled it with water for him. He also offered Speer "a drink of good whiskey which you Know I took a harty one." Later the same man let the exhausted captive ride his horse.[9]

Speer was at Governor's Island less than a month before being transferred to Johnson's Island. The route took him and his fellow prisoners through Buffalo and Cleveland. Along the way large crowds turned out to get a look at the live Confederates. "Some places there might have been 800 or 1,000 people to see us," Speer recorded. "It was amusing to see how foolish the people would act & do when the car Stoped." Some conceded that the Rebels were "good looking men." Others suggested that they be hanged or shouted, "Let's cut their throats." When they reached the prison the captives received a different kind of greeting. On both sides of the Mason-Dixon Line, newly arrived prisoners were known as "fresh fish." The veteran prisoners were always anxious to learn if the newcomers were members of their old outfit and to hear the latest news from the fighting front. When Speer and his fellow prisoners entered the Johnson's Island compound, "We were soon surrounded by hundreds of secesh officers all anxious to See who we were & if they Knew any of us." The Tar Heel soldier sadly noted that he did not recognize anybody among the approximately 1,300 prisoners on the island.[10]

Another Governor's Island prisoner who arrived at Johnson's Island on June 21 was Edward William Drummond. An enlisted clerk, Drummond had been captured with the headquarters staff at Fort Pulaski, a Georgia coastal fortification, on April 11. Union officials apparently assumed he was an officer, which explains why he ended up at Johnson's Island. Drummond's diary entries concerning the transfer largely match Speer's account. "It seems that the news was sent ahead of us on the road and at every Depot the place was crowded with eager eyes, all anxious to see a Secesh," he wrote. Like Speer he noted that the Confederates "received a great many compliments" but also "had to swallow a great many insults."[11]

Upon arrival Drummond's party, like all prisoners, had to turn their money over to Major Pierson. "Our Money was all taken away from us when we arrived and is in the Commander's hands," he explained, "and anything we buy we check on him for he is a regular Bank and has checks printed for the purpose." Drummond and fellow Block 5 captives arrived with enough funds to eat well, despite the fact that the sutler "charges about Four prices." They also had enough money to hire three lieutenants as cooks. Each chipped in twenty-five cents a week for the luxury. The money went quickly, however, and after only about two weeks on the island, Drummond observed, "all hands are getting along very comfortably, but if we stay here much longer we shall have to come down to Government Rations, as all our funds are getting rather low."[12]

Guy was more concerned over the "want of some mental stimulant." At all Union prisons many captives found their surroundings to be both bustling and boring. "When I read it is with the hum of conversation & the ring of laughter in my ear," he complained while still at Camp Chase. "When I walk it is to receive & return the bow of an acquaintance at one step, to elbow my way through a knot of strangers at the next, to avoid the advances of some bore at the next, to dodge contact with some dirty looking wretch who looks as if he had some contagious disease at the next & so encountering at every movement some interruption to continued thought." He voiced similar complaints at Johnson's Island, describing a pair of prisoners in his block as "two very disagreeable companions." Fortunately for Guy, he had the means to purchase a number of books, even if he had difficulty finding a quiet place to enjoy them. One shipment he received from a Cincinnati firm included fifty-seven volumes. The order cost him one hundred dollars in Confederate money.[13]

Newspapers were highly prized as reading matter among the prisoners, and Johnson's Island was one of the few pens where they were allowed to receive them. As June came to an end, the Confederates were particularly anxious to read reports of the Seven Days Battles going on in front of Richmond. The battles were the culmination of Gen. George McClellan's campaign to capture the Confederate capital by advancing up the peninsula formed by the York and James Rivers. They also marked the emergence of Robert E. Lee as a force to be reckoned with by Union generals.

On June 30 the *Register* printed an extra giving an account of the early fighting. Prisoners stood on stumps and read the report to eager crowds. "The hurrah in the prison over it was immense," Guy wrote. Speer added, "I never have seen as Lively & no[i]sy [a] time." According to Drummond, the celebration continued inside the blocks well after taps was sounded. "We sang, danced, cheered and felt merry generally," he observed. Not everyone was so amused. The next day both Drummond and Andrew Jackson Campbell wrote that Major Pierson claimed that it had been difficult for him to restrain the sentinels from firing into the happy crowds. Reports continued to trickle in. They were less than specific, but on July 8 Captain Guy concluded, "We have made up our minds that McClellan has met with a terrible repulse at Richmond, but the northern papers will not admit it." It was a generally accurate assessment.[14]

Being imprisoned on an island brought a few advantages. The biggest was the opportunity to bathe in the lake. Drummond termed the activity "a luxury not at all to be done away with." He did complain, however, when an excursion boat passed the island and the women on the deck ogled the men "and were not at all embarrassed." Speer was even more annoyed when two boats with black passengers passed the island. "O! how the black Bucks & wentches laugh at us," he wrote. Occasionally those same boats brought cheers from the Confederates. On at least two occasions the band on board struck up "Dixie," once interrupting "Yankee Doodle" to honor the prisoners' request for their national air. At other times the entertainment was more mundane. "We have today had an opportunity of watching the process of mowing with a machine," Drummond noted on July 18, "a sight unseen by many a one here before."[15]

The prisoners engaged in a variety of outdoor activities. "I had never realized the truth of the saying that men are nothing but grown-up boys until I was taken prisoner," Campbell observed. "Since that time I have seen more of the boy shown in men than I ever saw before." Marbles and "pitching quotes" were among the games played. Occasionally the prisoners staged sham battles. One of the most popular amusements was the game prisoner Richard L. Gray referred to as "town ball" and Drummond termed "base ball." On July 5 the prisoners from Fort Pulaski challenged a team selected from the rest of the captives. There were eleven players on each squad. "They beat us considerably," Drummond, a member of the Fort Pulaski team, wrote, "which was no more than we expected as they had a great advantage in the selection."[16]

Indoor pastimes included checkers, backgammon, chess, and a variety of card games. Although Gray wrote that the prisoners studied mathematics, history, chemistry, and other subjects, Guy complained that, "Not one in ten in all the prison ever reads and it is not for want of books." When not reading himself, Guy enjoyed listening to a group of singers in his block. As the summer wore on, autograph collecting became a popular activity. "I don't know how many times I have written my name in the last few days," Guy noted on August 2.[17]

The greatest number of captives occupied their time by making a variety of items. "Nearly everybody is making rings & various other articles for Keepsakes and also to help pass away time," Drummond wrote. Although this observation was accurate as far as it went, the activity was more than a pastime. As prisoners began to run out of money, the selling of homemade trinkets gave them a source of income and a way to supplement their government-issued rations.[18]

For Speer the resourcefulness of the Confederate captives was a source of pride. "I believe the Southern men can beet [sic] the yankees to death on inventions & tricks when necessity requires that they shall put their hands, minds, & wits to work," he proudly observed. Other Confederate diarists confirmed that opinion, at least in terms of the variety of products turned out by the prisoners. Canes, furniture, chess sets, and pipes were among the items produced, and knives were the principal tool. Some of the craftsmen converted case knives into saws, and others managed to secure files and chisels. One of Richard Gray's messmates had a bench in the block and continued his prewar profession of making boots and shoes. Gray himself had a monopoly on cigar making. In two months he realized nearly fifty dollars from the occupation. An engineer officer made drawings of the camp and its buildings, which he sold for a dollar apiece. Campbell wrote that there were some six or seven tailors in the compound who were kept busy seven days a week. Prisoners lacking skills but willing to work took in laundry. The largest group of launderers, composed of Virginians, reportedly washed as many as 140 pieces some days.[19]

By far the most common vocation was jewelry making. Prisoners made rings from gutta percha, a hard, rubberlike resin. Guy claimed that over half of the Johnson's Island captives were thus employed. Some received the raw material from friends outside the prison, and some converted gutta percha buttons into rings. Those with friends were also able to secure gold or silver for settings. Those without used pieces of shell they found while bathing in the lake. Even the prickly Guy admitted that "some of them [the rings] are very neat, ingenious & tasty." Breast pins, shirt buttons, and watch fobs were also produced by prison jewelry makers.[20]

Upon his arrival at Johnson's Island, William Speer received warnings from the veteran prisoners about trigger-happy guards. On two occasions, the "fresh fish" was informed, sentinels had fired into the blocks, wounding men severely. Although surviving camp records do not mention any shooting incidents during Johnson's Island's early months as a prison facility, Andrew Jackson Campbell dutifully recorded five. The first three occurred before the other prison diarists arrived. The last two were confirmed by his fellow prisoners. The first shooting mentioned by Campbell took place on May 21. The victim was a prisoner who was found outside his block after 10:00 p.m. Eight days later Campbell wrote, "A prisoner at the well with a bucket just after dark was shot in the leg." He offered no further details about the incident.[21]

The next shooting Campbell recorded was also reported by the *Register*. It happened on June 13. According to the Tennesseean, the prisoner, a captain, was shot through both legs above the knees. Once again Campbell supplied no details but wrote that it was "an attempt on the part of the sentinel to murder in cold blood." Two days later Campbell claimed that the guard had received "many presents" from the citizens of Sandusky for his act. This seems unlikely, since news of the incident had probably not reached Sandusky this quickly. He also wrote that the *Register* had falsely claimed that the victim had disobeyed orders. In reality the local paper was criticized for appearing to take the prisoner's side. In its June 19 account of the incident, the *Register* ran the victim's denial that he was in violation of any rules. The paper added, "It is a matter of regret that a prisoner should have been injured when there was any doubt of his propriety." This produced an angry response from a member of the Hoffman Battalion, who felt the account suggested that "the Battalion do not strictly obey orders given them." The *Register* denied that this was its intent, adding, "We have heard no intimation, from any quarter, of disobedience to orders on the part of the members of the Battalion, and our item was not intended to imply any."[22]

On August 9 Campbell wrote, "Last night another cold-blooded murder was committed by a villainous yankee sentinel." On this occasion three other diarists—all of them Confederate—basically corroborated his account of what had transpired. Lt. Elijah Gibson, an Arkansas prisoner, was killed after being shot through the chest. Gibson was returning to his block sometime between 9:30 and 10:30 P.M. after visiting friends in another barracks. A sentinel spotted the prisoner and ordered him to return to his block. After replying that he was doing just that, the lieutenant continued on. At that point the guard ordered him to turn around and go back. Gibson complied, but as he attempted to enter the block he was passing, the guard fired. Some time passed before anyone was allowed to go to his aid. By the time assistance arrived, he was dead. Speer agreed that it was "cold willful and premeditated murder." Even the more understated Drummond termed the incident "a most melancholy and cowardly proceeding."[23]

At midnight or shortly after on July 20, two shots alerted the Johnson's Island prisoners. They later learned that a group of captives had crawled through a ditch to one of the walls as part of an escape attempt. As they attempted to pull off one the planks, the noise alerted one of the guards, who quickly arrived and fired the shots as the men retreated toward their quarters. No one was hit, and the prison officials apparently never learned the identities of the guilty parties.[24]

The incident of July 20 was apparently the only escape attempt made on the island during 1862. Monthly prison reports, first made in July 1862, show no escapes for the year. Despite that, Pierson became very concerned that the prisoners were formulating a "concerted plan for general revolt with a view of taking the island and take their chances for escape." He informed Hoffman of this concern on June 18 and requested an additional company of guards. Pierson also asked that a group of prisoners "who exert a very bad influence" be sent to Fort Warren, an extremely secure facility in Boston Harbor. The next day Pierson sent a follow-up message, claiming that a plot was being formulated by Southern sympathizers in Canada to release the prisoners.[25]

The ironclad steamer *Michigan* provided security at Johnsons' Island. (Courtesy Massachusetts MOLLUS Collection, United States Army Military History Institute, Carlisle Barracks, Pa.)

One week after sending this message, Pierson again claimed that a scheme for the release of the prisoners was afoot. This time the commandant cited a source, a Confederate surgeon who had recently been sent away under Union orders to release all medical officers. The doctor claimed that the leaders were desperate and were likely to make the attempt even if the chances of success were slim. He told Pierson that they were determined to tear down the fences or buildings and fashion rafts to get across the lake to the mainland. Hoffman replied that the scheme was "scarcely within the range of possibility," but he did take action. The commissary general persuaded Governor Tod to send a company from Columbus to reinforce the garrison and counseled Pierson that he must institute a "thorough system of drill" for the arriving soldiers. He also offered some advice for dealing with unruly prisoners. "Kindness alone will not keep prisoners in subjection," he wrote, "and when you can single out a turbulent character you must resort to severe measures."[26]

Tod, who liked to sign his correspondence "Governor and Commander in Chief," went further than Hoffman requested. In addition to dispatching a company to Sandusky, he asked Secretary of the Navy Gideon Welles to send the steamer *Michigan* to reinforce the island. The United States Navy's first ironclad, built in 1844, it was the only vessel patrolling Lake

Erie. Before Tod's request came in it had seen service in the waters near Buffalo and Cleveland. Ironically, it would eventually become part of just the type of plot Pierson feared.[27]

It soon appeared that it would not be necessary for Rebel prisoners to hatch escape plots in order to return to Dixie. As the Confederate officers spent the spring and summer of 1862 at Johnson's Island, officials from the North and the South were moving toward an agreement for exchanging prisoners. The negotiations were both complicated and contentious. They were hindered by President Abraham Lincoln's desire to avoid any recognition of the Confederacy. They were encouraged by Northern public opinion, which cared more about brothers, sons, husbands, and fathers who were languishing in Southern prisons. Thousands of captives, Union and Confederate, were caught in the middle of all of this. They only wanted to go home. Soon they would, as Civil War prison history entered a humane but temporary phase.

3

"Everything in Prison Is Elated"

The Road to Exchange

The practice of paroling prisoners of war in the Civil War actually pre-dated the official start of the conflict. Such was the case with Hoffman and his comrades in Texas, whom the Confederates paroled before the guns sounded at Fort Sumter. As the armies headed into the field, generals occasionally made informal, temporary exchange agreements. The deals were more problematic for Union generals, who had to be careful to sustain the Lincoln administration's policy of avoiding any official recognition of the Confederacy. In October 1861 General Grant returned three captured Confederates to the Southern lines. In doing so, he was careful to make clear to Leonidas Polk, the opposing general, "I recognize no Southern Confederacy myself." He pointedly ordered the officer who conducted the captives back to their lines to "avoid all discussions upon the rights of belligerents."[1]

In the Eastern Theater the greatest number of early exchanges were made by Maj. Gen. John E. Wool, the Union commander at Fortress Monroe, Virginia, and Maj. Gen. Benjamin Huger of the Confederate Department of Norfolk. The process, which began during the fall of 1861, at first involved small numbers and was limited to members of the navy and the marine corps. The numbers gradually grew, but seldom reached a hundred at a time. Perhaps the most bizarre practice involved releasing Confederates on parole and sending them south to obtain the release of Union prisoners of equal rank, thus securing their own exchange. In late 1861 some 250 Fort Warren prisoners made the journey. The practice continued for some six months. It ended when the parolees began ignoring the terms of their release and simply headed for home instead.[2]

Although individual exchanges continued to be arranged, the administration's phobia concerning recognition of the Confederacy precluded any general agreement on the subject of exchange. Still, there were practical limits to a policy of obstinacy. One presented itself when the crew of the captured Confederate privateer *Jeff Davis* was convicted of piracy and sentenced to death. The real Jefferson Davis, president of the Confederacy, sent word through the lines that an equal number of Union prisoners had been selected for the same punishment. For both humane and political considerations, Lincoln quietly set aside the sentence.[3]

It was the latter that eventually led Lincoln and Secretary of War Stanton to relent as well on the general subject of exchange. By 1862 public pressure had grown strong for an exchange cartel. Both Congress and state legislatures passed resolutions calling upon the president to "inaugurate systematic measures for the exchange of prisoners." On February 11 Stanton abruptly informed Wool that "you alone are clothed with full powers for the purpose of arranging for the exchange of prisoners." Meeting with Gen. Howell Cobb of the Confederate Army, Wool attempted to do so. Stanton, however, objected to the wording of the agreement that resulted and rejected it outright.[4]

This was not the end of the matter. On June 23 the Senate passed another resolution. The same day the *New York Times,* a paper friendly to Lincoln, editorialized, "Our government must change its policy, our prisoners must be exchanged!" Lincoln and Stanton were out of time. Any further delay brought with it great political risk. Realizing that, on July 12 Stanton instructed Maj. Gen. John Dix to "negotiate a general exchange of prisoners with the enemy." Two days later Gen. Robert E. Lee ordered Maj. Gen. Daniel Harvey Hill to meet with Dix to consummate the deal.[5]

Following a series of meetings at Haxall's Landing on the James River, the two generals reached an agreement on July 22. It was based closely upon a similar exchange cartel used by the United States and Great Britain during the War of 1812. It established a sliding scale to calculate the relative value of enlisted men and officers of various ranks. Each belligerent was to appoint an agent of exchange, and the two were to oversee the process. Any disputes were to be "made the subject of friendly explanations in order that the object of this agreement may neither be defeated nor postponed." Charges and countercharges would soon render this passage moot.[6]

At Johnson's Island rumors of an impending exchange began to circulate nearly a month before the Dix-Hill Cartel was signed. "We have had some news about an immediate exchange but put no confidence in anything," William Drummond wrote on June 24. Four days later the rumors had been "all knocked in the head." One day after that he noted that the prospects for exchange now seemed likely. Meanwhile, Drummond looked for some positive evidence. He believed he had found some on July 14, when he learned that prison officials were preparing lists of prisoners. A more certain sign came on the 17th as a report circulated that the camp commissary had orders to cease purchases, "as the number here would be greatly reduced in a few days." Drummond added, "This news does not come through the grape vine, but direct from head quarters."[7]

When exchange became official, it did not take long for the news to reach the Lake Erie prison. "Papers state positively that arrangements at last have been completed between Genls. Hill & Dix . . . for an immediate exchange of prisoners," Guy wrote on July 24. He added, "Everything in Prison is elated." Added Drummond, "All hands have been in a high state of excitement all day over the good news." The next day he wrote that some were buying carpet bags and trunks, and a few had gone so far as to pack for the anticipated trip. The majority, however, had resolved to trust no reports "until we are across the line and under our own glorious flag."[8]

Not all prisoners were elated at the prospect of exchange, and at some camps a number of them chose not to pack for a return trip to Dixie. Some offered to take an oath of allegiance to the Union. Others simply wished to give their parole of honor to remain in the North and not support the Confederacy. Governor Tod claimed that several Camp Chase captives begged him to "protect them against unconditional exchange." The number of prospective oath takers varied from camp to camp. The largest number appeared to come from Tennessee, a state where loyalties were decidedly divided. Union officials tried to take advantage of the ambivalence of the Volunteer State soldiers by dispatching Andrew Johnson, the loyalist war governor of Tennessee, and a number of other speakers to the Midwestern camps. How many were converted is difficult to determine, but the number was likely low.[9]

The oath was particularly unpopular among the Southern officers at Johnson's Island. On August 10 camp officials posted notices reading, "Prisoners who prefer taking the Oath of Allegiance to going South to join the Southern Army will apply to Maj. Pierson immediately. By order." According to Campbell, the prisoners tore down the posters as soon as they went up. Soon, "Old Person [Pierson] immediately sent in and had the bills posted around the walls so the sentinels could keep them from being torn down."[10]

On July 9 Drummond had heard of one man taking the oath. "I wish we had his name," he wrote at the time. "He should be recollected." By the time the notices went up, Drummond was less concerned. Learning that the posters had attracted only two oath takers, he noted, "Those that wish to do it we are satisfied to let go as they are of no use to us." He added with apparent satisfaction, "The Yankees seem surprised that their flaming announcement is not more fully appreciated." On August 27 John Guy placed the number of oath takers at five. He added that three of them were native Northerners and one was of foreign birth.[11]

At all camps the vast majority of Confederate captives preferred exchange to the oath. Since the Union at this time held in excess of 17,000 prisoners at its major depots, this created a daunting logistical challenge. Two sites were designated as points of exchange. For Eastern prisoners it was Aiken's Landing, Virginia, on the James River. Captives from Western pens, including Johnson's Island, would head for Vicksburg, Mississippi. On August 26 Hoffman sent instructions to Major Pierson for the exchange process. The Confederates were to depart at 6:00 A.M. on the 29th. One company would go with them as guards, and the departing prisoners were to be provided with three days' rations. Hoffman added, "You will instruct the commander of the guard to be very careful that none of his charge escape by the way and that they are not interfered with in any way at stopping places on the route." The Johnson's Island guards would accompany the prisoners only as far as Cairo, Illinois. From there a detail from the Cairo post would travel with the Confederates down the Mississippi to Vicksburg.[12]

The Johnson's Island prisoners were scheduled to depart on September 1. The day before they were to leave, Guy's diary entry was brief: "This is our last day here. No reading, no writing, no anything to day, but bustle & expectation." According to Drummond, the prisoners were doubtful about the news until about 11:00 A.M., when Pierson himself came into the compound to announce the impending departure. "No one can picture our delight and the delight of our whole party and I feel the enjoyment," he confided to his diary, adding, "All hands are sitting around tonight and are ready. The moments will pass away very slow."[13]

The prisoners were delivered to Sandusky the next morning in the steamers *Island Queen* and *Little Eastern*. It was a slow process, and according to the *Register,* the last of the captives did not leave the city until two o'clock that afternoon. "It required two long trains to transport them and their luggage, of which there was no small amount," the paper reported. As they waited the prisoners engaged in "a very brisk trade" with people selling apples, cigars, and newspapers. "Even some 'fire water' found its way into the canteens and bottles of the secesh," the *Register* asserted, "although the guard attempted to prevent the smuggling in of the ardent." The departing Rebels attracted a large crowd of curious citizens, although the delay was such that few remained by the time the trains started south.[14]

As they headed for Vicksburg, the entries of the Johnson's Island diarists became less regular. None were able to write during the railroad journey to Cairo. Gray later noted that the prisoners rode in passenger cars as far as Indianapolis and were then transferred to boxcars and cattle cars. On this latter leg of the trip, they waited an hour or more at various stations until higher-priority trains passed. When this happened, the prisoners were allowed to visit local stores. Gray was pleased to report that he discovered much pro-Southern sentiment along the route from Indianapolis to Cairo. The trains reached Cairo between 10:00 and 11:00 P.M. on September 3.[15]

Upon reaching the Illinois city, the prisoners were marched to the wharf, placed aboard a steamer, and towed out to the middle of the Mississippi. This proved to be the worst part of the trip. "There are now about Five Thousand here and there are Five large boats laying in the River crowded and all faring hard," Drummond wrote. Rations were raw, and there was no way to cook them. The water, which came from the river, was, according to Gray, "warm and very unpalatable." The only consolation, the Virginian pointed out, was the scenery. "The view at night of Cairo in the moon light with the numerous steamers at wharf and anchored in stream with their lights is to me grand & beautiful," he observed.[16]

On September 8 the flotilla started down the Mississippi. Ten steamers, including a gun boat and a hospital boat, began the last leg of the journey that was to return the prisoners to the Confederacy. The atmosphere changed quickly. "All along as we go down the River the Ladies along the Banks and at different towns wave their handkerchiefs and Hurrah for Jeff Davis, which we return with hearty good cheers." According to Gray, the men reserved their loudest cheers for the wife of one of the prisoners, whose affecting story "makes my heart well up and chokes utterance & speech." She appeared with a small group along the river bank, near the couple's home. Somehow she learned that her husband was aboard, and somehow the two managed to make contact. The woman was able to inform him that "all was well and doing well." As the boats went around a large bend in the river, she left their view. She reappeared, however, around the bend, having ridden six miles across the peninsula. This prompted the cheers from the inspired Confederates. "In her were evidenced the beautiful Virtues of womanly devotion, constancy, and Patriotism," Gray enthused, "swiftly galloping her steed, her white handkerchief streaming."[17]

Memphis, where the boats took on coal, was another highlight for the prisoners. Local women came out in skiffs and other small craft to distribute food to the Confederates. As his boat anchored at the shore, a Camp Douglas prisoner wrote, "Multitudes of wimmin crouded around and hallowd for Jeff Davis and the South. Tha give meny Gifts of tobaco apples and peaches candy and all sorts of grappess. The boys gave them Rings in return whitch was verry acceptable with the Tenn Girles." The most beautiful sight, however, was Vicksburg, where the men stepped again onto Southern soil. Many met friends, and all enjoyed the "extensive preparations for eating & lodging" made for them by local residents.[18]

According to the *Register,* the prisoners had also made extensive preparations for their return to the Confederate Army before leaving Sandusky. "The report is current," the paper wrote on September 5, "that the rebel prisoners of war, when they left here on Monday last, were bountifully provided with clothing which they purchased here." It was rumored that they had even secured Confederate uniforms, "which were flaunted in the faces of our citizens." The reports eventually made their way to Levi C. Turner, the associate judge-advocate for the District of Columbia. He informed Stanton that the prisoners had departed with 500 gray uniforms. Turner further asserted that the Confederates' baggage had not been inspected before they left the prison. A guard force was later dispatched, Turner's report continued, which overtook the trains and recovered about a carload of blankets, shoes, and other federal property. Hoffman demanded a report, backed by affidavits, from Pierson. The commandant's reply, which apparently was later lost, satisfied the commissary general. He reported to Adj. Gen. Lorenzo Thomas that Pierson provided "abundant proof" that "the charges came from men without any reliable character and are without the slightest foundation."[19]

As exchange continued and the Northern prisons emptied, Hoffman made plans to consolidate the remaining captives. On August 11 he informed Pierson that Johnson's Island would house any that were left after the exchange process. He urged the major to get in a winter's supply of wood. On September 9 Hoffman ordered the commander at Camp Douglas to forward any remaining prisoners to Sandusky. The same day the war department directed that all political prisoners, except those whose cases were being investigated at Camp Chase, also be dispatched to Johnson's Island. When a detachment of three hundred arrived from the Alton Prison in mid-November, Pierson complained that they were "in wretched condition. About fifty had to go to the hospital at once," he continued, "and without stopping to be accurate I should think eight or ten have died, more than unusual for two months."[20]

After peaking at 1,462 on August 31, Johnson's Island's prison population declined drastically. One month later it was at 822. By March 1863 the number was down to 106. It bottomed out two months later at 40.[21]

Although few in number, the prisoners confined at Johnson's Island during this period included some of the most controversial of the war. Likely because of its remote and secure location, the depot became the site for a number of military executions resulting from courts martial. Although at least one of the sentences was later commuted, four were carried out on the island. There likely would have been more executions there had Hoffman not intervened. During the fall of 1863, Gen. Ambrose Burnside, then commanding the Department of the Ohio, ordered several prisoners facing death sentences to the Sandusky depot. The commissary general informed him that Johnson's Island did not have sufficient facilities to house them all and requested that he find another site.[22]

The first executions at Johnson's Island occurred on May 15, 1863. The condemned were William F. Corbin and T. G. McGraw, both Kentucky residents. A military commission that met in Cincinnati on April 22 convicted them of recruiting for the Confederate Army in Pendleton County, Kentucky, within the Union lines. Members of the Hoffman Battalion carried out the sentence. The prisoners rode to the scene of the execution, on the south side of the island, in a wagon, seated upon their coffins. They were then placed in front of those same boxes, the squad of sixteen soldiers fired, and the two men fell dead into their coffins.[23]

The next person executed at Johnson's Island was a Union soldier. Reuben Stout of the 60th Indiana Volunteer Infantry had been convicted of desertion and murder at a court-martial held in Indianapolis. The twenty-eight-year-old had deserted and then shot Solomon Huffman, who was attempting to arrest him for desertion. Stout insisted that Huffman had threatened to shoot him and that he had fired in self-defense. The court was unmoved. It found Stout guilty and sentenced him to death.[24]

By the time of the execution on October 23, 1863, the Confederate prison population at Johnson's Island was again growing. At least three prisoners mentioned the proceedings in their diaries, although they gave it only brief attention. One noted that the prisoners were not allowed outside their blocks as the sentence was carried out. Another complained, "The execution could not be seen well from our block." As the war continued, the prisoners would have two more opportunities to view such spectacles.[25]

The reason that the number of Confederates was increasing at Johnson's Island was the collapse of the exchange cartel. Almost from the outset, charges and countercharges had flown across the Mason-Dixon Line from both directions. Indeed, the executions of Corbin and McGraw at Johnson's Island entered into the picture. Confederate officials demanded the records of the case and threatened to select two Union captains to execute in retaliation "for this gross barbarity." Union authorities responded by threatening to execute an equal number of Confederate officers if the Southerners carried out their threat.[26]

It was another execution that started events in motion that eventually made the cartel a dead letter. In June 1862, Gen. Benjamin Butler, the Union's military governor of Louisiana, hanged a New Orleans man who allegedly tore down a U.S. flag. The Confederates responded by refusing to exchange Union officers, and the Union responded to that action by refusing to return Confederate officers to the South. Individual exchanges of officers were later resumed, but any number of contentious issues continued to plague the efforts of Union and Confederate negotiators.

The disagreement that finally doomed the cartel was the issue of black soldiers and their white officers. On May 1, 1863, the Confederate congress responded to President Lincoln's Emancipation Proclamation and the Union's decision to accept black soldiers into the army. The Southern legislators passed a resolution declaring that officers leading black troops into battle were to be "deemed as inciting servile insurrection." If captured, they would be put to death. The men serving under them would be turned over to the states and presumably returned to slavery. Stanton responded by halting exchanges on July 13. William H. Ludlow, the Union's commissioner of exchange, protested the action and was promptly fired.[27]

The question of the Union's sincerity has long been debated by historians. Stanton's action came at a time when recent victories at Gettysburg and Vicksburg had given the Union a tremendous advantage in the number of prisoners. The North already had a substantial advantage in population, meaning exchange would benefit the Confederacy much more than the Union. General Grant, whose stock had risen even higher after taking Vicksburg, famously held this view. There is, however, no direct evidence that Union officials were insincere in their claims that the South's refusal to exchange black troops was the main factor in the collapse of the cartel. Further, since the South never budged on its rigid position, the North's sincerity was never put to the test. What is clear is that captives in both blue and gray were once again caught in the middle of the politicians' squabbles. For the thousands destined for Johnson's Island and other prisons, this meant their stays in a hostile land were likely to be both lengthy and unpleasant.

4

"It Requires Only Proper Energy and Judgment"

The Second Wave of Prisoners

The collapse of the cartel was quickly followed by waves of new prisoners destined for Johnson's Island and other Union prison camps. By August 1863 the Confederate population at the Sandusky depot was again over 2,000. It would remain between that figure and 2,600 for much of the rest of the war, exceeding 3,000 for the first time in December 1864.[1]

The exchange cartel likely saved the lives of thousands of prisoners, Union and Confederate, who would have otherwise languished in captivity for an additional two to three years. Unfortunately, its failure meant that conditions would be worse for most of the new prisoners suddenly heading north. Believing the cartel was the solution to the government's prison crisis, Hoffman and other officials did nothing to address maintenance needs at the Northern depots. In September 1862 the commissary general had predicted that Camp Chase would soon be abandoned. That same month he ordered that guards at the Columbus facility, as well as Camp Douglas and Camp Butler in Illinois, be mustered out when their terms of service expired "or when no longer necessary." As a result the Union was little better prepared to receive the flood of prisoners that arrived in 1863 than it had been to accommodate Grant's 1862 captives. Hoffman had no choice but to press the old depots into service again. Soon he added new facilities at Point Lookout, Maryland; Elmira, New York; and Rock Island, Illinois.

To a large degree, Johnson's Island avoided the problems that plagued other camps. Hoffman planned to keep open the prison he had built, intending it to serve as the sole depot in the west. As a result, the facility was well maintained during the period of exchange. Another advantage Johnson's Island benefited from was the fact that it did not serve as a parole camp during that same time. Soon after the cartel went into operation, Union officials—Stanton in particular—became concerned that soldiers were surrendering too willingly, hoping for a furlough home while waiting to be exchanged. The secretary of war addressed this issue by establishing parole camps. All paroled soldiers were required to report to these camps until exchanged. Among the facilities thus utilized were Camp Douglas and Camp Chase. They soon became home to thousands of unruly parolees, angry that their opportunity to visit their families had been suddenly snatched away. Many arrived without officers, and with little supervision they took out their frustrations on the dreary camps in which they found themselves. The damage was especially severe at Camp Douglas. There the parolees tore down much of the fence and were believed responsible for a fire that destroyed twelve buildings. Although the collapse of the cartel portended a lengthy stay for Confederates arriving at all Union prisons, those bound for Johnson's Island would at least reside at a depot physically prepared to receive them.[2]

Many of the prisoners headed for Johnson's Island began their journey at Gettysburg. When three days of fighting in and around the Pennsylvania village ended on July 3, 1863, the Union found itself with 13,621 prisoners, including 6,739 who had been wounded. Most ended up at Point Lookout, a prison established as a result of the battle. Many officers, however, continued on to Sandusky. Among them was John Dooley of the 1st Virginia Infantry, shot through both thighs as he followed Gen. George Pickett on his legendary charge against the center of the Union line on the final day of the battle. The next day he rode in a wagon with a wounded Yankee to a field hospital. "The whole ground for miles around is covered with the wounded, the dying and the dead," Dooley wrote of the scene.

Nine days later the Virginia officer boarded a train for Baltimore. His destination was Fort McHenry. The historic fortification served as a Union prison throughout the war, but it saw its greatest numbers during the weeks following Gettysburg, acting as a holding facility for captives destined for other prisons. While he was held there, Dooley slept on a filthy floor, dodging both rodents and vermin. The Union doctor was "most kind in his attentions." He was also kept busy. One day the physician removed four maggots from Dooley's wounds. A week later he extracted fabric from Dooley's pants that the bullet had carried into his wounds.[3]

By August 22 Dooley had recovered sufficiently to travel, and he joined a group of his fellow officers on a train bound for Sandusky. Following a long layover in Pittsburgh, where large crowds turned out to view the Rebels, the train reached the shores of Lake Erie at noon on the 24th. There was apparently also a crowd at Sandusky. Dooley wrote, "People here less sympathetic and meaner looking, if possible, than in Pittsburg." Two hours later a tug delivered Dooley and his comrades to the island. Upon arriving, the "fresh fish" were delayed for several hours in a drizzling rain while prison officials ordered them to turn over all their money, then searched them to make sure they had done so.[4]

Edmund DeWitt Patterson of the 9th Alabama Infantry was captured during the second day's fighting at Gettysburg. Patterson was not wounded, and the next day he joined some six hundred fellow captives on a thirty-nine-mile march to Westminster, Maryland. Although the Union officer in command did all he could to make the prisoners comfortable, they still suffered from hunger and heat. They spent the night in a stock pen and were jammed into cattle cars the next morning for the trip to Fort McHenry. Two days later he was sent to Fort Delaware, a Union prison on an island in the Delaware River. "A respectable hog would have turned up his nose in disgust at it," Patterson wrote of the facility, which is considered to have been one of the Union's worst prisons.[5]

On July 16 Patterson and his fellow officers learned that they would soon be sent to Johnson's Island. "This is glorious news to us," he wrote, "for we are anxious to go anywhere (except to Hell and some even said they would prefer the aforementioned place for the same length of time) in preference to remaining here." They departed two days later, passed through Philadelphia, Harrisburg, and Pittsburgh, and arrived at Sandusky on the 20th. Greeting their train at Sandusky was a vocal crowd of men, women, and children. They welcomed the captives by shouting such things as "You might have known that we could whip you," and "We will teach you how to rebel against the best government under the sun." Patterson found a measure of satisfaction by noting in his diary that "not one in a thousand of them was ever near enough to a battle to hear the thunder."[6]

The summer of 1863 also witnessed the arrival of a number of prisoners from the Western theater. General Grant paroled the men surrendered at Vicksburg on July 4, but those taken five days later at Port Hudson, Louisiana, were not so fortunate. Among them were Capt. Thomas Jones Taylor of the 49th Alabama Infantry and Maj. J. L. Stockdale, who was in charge of the commissary department at the fortification. On the 16th Taylor boarded the steamer *Planet* for the trip up the Mississippi, and Stockdale started north two days later. Both officers were discouraged by the sights they encountered as their boats continued up the river. "We saw along the river bank not a single cultivated farm, not a single farm house inhabited, scarcely a horse, cow, or other domestic animal," Taylor observed. "Many of their tasteful residences had been burned, the negroes carried or driven off, and all vestiges of life actually obliterated." Stockdale agreed, noting, "The farms on the bank of the river is a desolate waste, not one under cultivation, the houses either burned or vacated, not a living thing to be seen except here and there a negro."[7]

At Cairo the prisoners boarded trains for the remainder of their journey to Johnson's Island. If their accounts are accurate, the two Confederate officers had somewhat different experiences during this phase of the trip. Taylor wrote that, although crowds gathered at every stop, "we were not insulted in a single instance by anyone in the garb or appearance of a lady or gentleman." However, according to Stockdale, "the natives stared at us like [we] were wild beasts." He added, "The females especially were eager to see us and took every means to show us they were rejoiced at our misfortunes and hated rebels." With few exceptions, Taylor felt the guards "were very civil." Stockdale and his comrades encountered one kind lieutenant, who let the prisoners go to a hotel for breakfast during a layover at Indianapolis. When his superiors learned of the generosity, they placed the lieutenant under arrest and confined the Confederates to the guard house until they departed the city. Taylor reached Johnson's Island on July 28, Stockdale the next day. Both were subjected to searches before being ushered into the compound.[8]

For Virgil Murphey, who was captured more than a year later, the journey to Johnson's Island was considerably worse. Murphey was taken prisoner on November 30, 1864, at the Battle of Franklin, in Tennessee. He was taken to nearby Nashville, where he shared a cramped penitentiary cell with sixty-seven other officers. Promised rations never arrived. "It was a long wretched night," Murphey later wrote, "the most miserable of my life and will remain in my memory as a monument to Yankee hardness of heart." On December 2 Murphey and his comrades boarded boxcars for Louisville. Guarding them was the 173rd Ohio Infantry, an outfit that he termed "the most blasphemous vulgar and disgusting ruffians I ever met." They were, Murphey wrote, "cowardly in their instincts, brutal in their treatment and blustering and hectoring in their demeanor." This was an unusual observation. Prisoners generally spoke highly of the guards who accompanied them from the front. Murphey attributed this alleged attitude of the 173rd to his claim that the regiment had abandoned its position in the battle and was applying "a salve to their wounded vanity by wreaking vengeance upon their defenseless opponents."[9]

At Louisville, Union guards confiscated the prisoners' knives. On a more positive note, stoves helped take away the chill of the cold railroad ride. Their stay was brief. A few hours after arriving, the captives were conducted across the Ohio and again found themselves in freight cars, this time bound for Indianapolis. Murphey and comrades changed cars at the Indiana capital. They reached Sandusky during the night of December 6 and immediately boarded ferries for Johnson's Island. The prisoners were subjected to the usual search, a process made far worse by their introduction to December on Lake Erie. "The night was bitter and intensely cold," Murphey wrote, "and the fierce north wind penetrated through our thin . . . garments as we were halted at the office of the prison commandant for examination."[10]

Once inside, cries of "fresh fish" greeted Murphey, along with numerous inquiries from prisoners starved for information. "I was literally besieged with questions," he wrote. Murphey learned that a number of his fellow Johnson's Island captives were friends and acquaintances. All were anxious for news about friends and loved ones at home. "I sat there and answered inquiries until 3 oclock notwithstanding my weariness . . . and desire for repose," he noted. "I cheered many disponding hearts and thank God I had no message of grief and woe for any of [the] almost forsaken prisoners." It was a scene repeated whenever a new group of captives arrived. The veteran prisoners were especially eager to receive reports from the fighting front. On one occasion, according to prison diarist William Peel of the 11th Mississippi Infantry, half a dozen "fresh fish" attracted an instant crowd. "The men called loudly for the news," Peel wrote. One of the newcomers was lifted onto a barrel, putting him in a difficult position since the barrel did not have a head on either end. Three men held him in place as other prisoners shouted for silence so any news could be heard. Before they could get the crowd quieted, a sentinel ordered everyone to disperse, and nothing was learned.[11]

Murphey's first impressions of his new home were less than positive. "A majority of the Blocks are well built, closely sealed and comfortable," he observed. However, those that were not well sealed were open to north-

A view of a portion of the prison from Lake Erie. (Courtesy Sandusky County Library, Sandusky, Ohio)

ern winds, and Murphey concluded, "The consideration of health does not enter into the arrangement where rebels are concerned." Thomas Taylor's original observations had been similarly mixed. "This place is said to be very healthy, and I am inclined to believe it is true in regard to the summer season," he wrote, "but from the vast expanse around the island . . . I incline to believe that it is a most uncongenial residence during the winter for the men of the Sunny South." Taylor concluded, "I do not think our lot is a hard one. True, the restraint upon our liberty and our humiliating position are galling to our pride, yet, under the circumstances we can not expect better treatment."[12]

For prisoners arriving from other facilities, Johnson's Island looked good by comparison. Following brief stays at Fort McHenry and Fort Delaware, Edmund Patterson wrote, "We all like Johnson's Island much better than any other [prison] we have found since leaving Dixie." His main reason for feeling that way was the fact that the captives had far less contact with their guards at the Lake Erie depot. "This place is a great improvement upon Fort Delaware," wrote Robert Bingham of the 44th North Carolina Infantry. He explained, "The enclosure is about 16 acres & one can go all about during the day. The view of the lake is pleasant—& the air pure—& the fare mostly good."[13]

As the second wave of Confederate prisoners arrived at Johnson's Island, Union officials made plans for their new charges. Hoffman was particularly concerned with having the depot ready for the next Lake Erie winter. On September 3, 1863, he informed Pierson that parole was apparently at an end "and you may therefore expect that as many [prisoners] will be sent to the island as the barracks can accommodate." The commandant was instructed to "immediately take steps to obtain such a supply of all necessary stores as will meet all demands during the winter." Later that month the commissary general felt it necessary to remind the inexperienced officer that "as it becomes colder the prisoners will require to be more warmly clad than heretofore." Those with funds would be permitted to purchase overcoats and underwear. Warm clothing could be provided to the others upon the recommendation of the medical officer.[14]

In early October Hoffman dispatched Dr. Augustus M. Clark to Johnson's Island. Clark was kept busy as Hoffman's primary medical inspector, venturing from camp to camp and sending back reports that were unsparing and thorough. He inspected the Lake Erie prison on October 7, reporting that it housed 2,233 prisoners, 16 Union officers, and 384 enlisted men. Clark found the policing of the camp to be "very good" in the Union quarters and hospital and "most inexcusably neglected" in the Confederate quarters and hospital. He gave the barracks high marks except for "very poor" ventilation. The sinks, Clark reported, were "filthy."

Dr. Woodbridge was still on duty as camp surgeon. Clark reported that he was "evidently a skillful practitioner of medicine but not well informed as to his military duties." He added, "The nurses (prisoners) are not kept up to their duties with sufficient strictness." As a result, "Some of the beds in the prisoners' hospital are in a terribly filthy condition; the bed pans not properly attended to; the floors show no evidence of ever having been cleansed." He added that hospital underclothing and bedding were "not properly washed." The inspector did not blame Dr. Woodbridge entirely. "It is utterly impossible for one officer to properly discharge all the duties required of him," Clark noted. "At least two more medical officers should be stationed here."

Dr. Clark made several other recommendations for the camp. The lack of policing, he noted, was largely the fault of the prisoners. Still, stricter discipline could remedy much of the problem. Only one pump was available for water. Clark called for more. Prison barracks were being policed weekly. Clark urged that this be done daily. He suggested that the hospital capacity, then at sixty prisoners, be doubled. Finally, "Receptacles for garbage and other offal from the cook-houses and barracks should be provided. Lime or some more powerful disinfecting agent should be used more freely."[15]

Clark's inspection was far less damning than those he submitted from other prisons. It nevertheless got Hoffman's attention, and he ordered Pierson to correct the problems immediately. "This is a state of things for which there can be no excuse," the commissary general fumed. "It requires only proper energy and judgment on the part of those in charge to insure favorable results." He quoted numerous passages from Clark's inspection report, then wrote, "I make these quotations to call your attention to the most conspicuous deficiencies, in the expectation that immediate measures will be taken to remedy the present unsatisfactory condition of your command." Remembering Pierson's lack of military experience, Hoffman concluded, "You have the authority in your own hands, and it is left to your discretion and judgment to use it in such way as to insure proper results."[16]

All of this apparently hurt Pierson's feelings, and he defended himself in a response to Hoffman. He claimed that barracks were policed daily. Clark, he continued, had made his inspection during rainy weather, explaining why the policing was not done the day he was there. The commandant pointed out that thirty sinks had been dug during his tenure. He did concede, "New sinks are dug, but old ones are readily filled up, it is true, before new ones are supplied." He insisted that there were "receptacles for garbage" in place, which were emptied daily. Pierson addressed the topic of clothes washing by writing that he had recently had a building put up "where some laundresses will live." The commandant concluded, "Perhaps I ought to add that with all the disposition of prisoners to complain there has never been the first complaint from a sick person or their friends or any Confederate surgeon of want of supplies or care."[17]

The commissary general of prisoners showed remarkable patience with Pierson, the commander who came as close as anyone to being Hoffman's protege. In responding, he ignored most of Pierson's responses to the inspection report but again lectured the youthful commandant on military protocol. "I have not time to give you minute instructions about the many matters which you mention in your letter," Hoffman replied. "The responsibility for the good condition of your command is entirely upon yourself and it is expected that you will not wait for instructions, but act on your own judgment, only asking for authority when it is not already in your hands."[18]

Caught in the middle of all this were the prisoners on Johnson's Island. For them, Hoffman and Pierson's concerns about protocol represented decisions that affected their daily lives. They were concerned far less with the theoretical than with the practical. After the exchange cartel collapsed, these challenges became all the more critical, as the prisoners realized their stays were going to be quite lengthy. Hunger and loneliness were to be their companions for many months, and the resourceful Confederates were quick to devise methods of battling both.

5

"This Horrid Life of Inactivity"
The Battle with Boredom

For the prisoners who arrived at Johnson's Island in 1863 and 1864, the complaints largely mirrored those of their earlier counterparts from Fort Donelson. High on the list were the twin problems of bustle and boredom. Virgil Murphey wrote that he "could neither study nor reflect [among] the immense crowding and congregating of the officers together." Edmund Patterson complained, "From morning until night it is the same, talking, reading, walking, playing all kinds of games, in doors and out, and there is not a spot within the walls of this prison to which one can go for quiet reflection and meditation." A fellow prisoner, James Mayo, wrote of "a perfect babel of voices," which he graphically described.

> In the room here all are talking at once. . . . Capt. Hunter walking with hands stuck deep in his pockets complaining of being sick. Capt. Bingham, walking up, places some letters in his chair and singing "Bonnie Blue Star." Col. Cantrell reading, on my right, Capt. Burwell smoking and standing in the middle of the room and looking as if he wanted something to do. . . . Lt. Mills coughs, so do several others, while several others spit and blow their noses.[1]

Along with all this activity came a boring sense of sameness. "Prison life is nearly the same day by day, with little variety or change," observed J. L. Stockdale. Writing to his brother, Thomas Gibbes Morgan complained of "this horrid life of inactivity and uselessness." John Joyes, a member of John Hunt Morgan's cavalry division, summed up the situation succinctly in his diary entry for October 23, 1864. "A quiet, dull, uninteresting kind of day—nothing to do and nothing to do it with."[2]

The frustration growing out of this boredom was likely a factor in the occasional fights that broke out in the compound. On November 12, 1863, Mayo observed an altercation between a Mississippi lieutenant and a Georgia captain. Both were injured. Four weeks later a colonel and a lieutenant went at it. "It is much to be regretted that officers cannot have their intercourse more amicable," Mayo observed, "especially when from the same Regiment and under such circumstances." A number of prisoners were involved in an August 1864 altercation. One of the participants, who was struck with a chair, suffered a broken jaw and a serious eye injury. An even more serious affair took place during the waning months of the war. "Saw a difficulty this morning between Lt. Harman Morgan & a fellow named Berry who claims to be an officer," Joyes wrote on February 10, 1865. Morgan came out of the incident with three stab wounds, and Berry "had his head badly bruised with a billet of wood." Joyes believed Morgan would recover from his wounds, but they proved fatal. In reporting the incident to General Grant, who was then the Union's general in chief, Hoffman described Berry as a civilian prisoner. Grant ordered that Berry's trial be held on the island, but the outcome is not known.[3]

The most effective remedy for the boredom and loneliness of prison life was the arrival of a letter from home. Until exchange was resumed late in the war, the announcement of a "Dixie mail" from a flag-of-truce boat was the most exciting notice the prisoners could receive. "Shut out from the benefits of good society and the influence of home, one finds but little enjoyment except in those silent messengers that come from home & friends," one prisoner wrote in a return letter. "With what anxiety we watch each day for the mail," he noted, "but when the mail comes while some are rejoicing over letters from home and friends, others are down cast with a 'What's the reason I dont get a letter?'" Upon receiving a letter from his sister, E. John Ellis of the 16th Louisiana Infantry wrote in his diary, "I would not swap it for Maximilian's sceptor and the patronage of Napoleon thrown in to boot."[4]

The prisoners' correspondence was subject to censorship. This was a time-consuming process, and for this reason letters were limited to a single page. The policy was the same at every camp, but at some, including Johnson's Island, the captives could get longer letters through for a financial consideration. "Have been writing some 'dime letters,' or in other words letters of four pages," Patterson wrote in a diary entry. "The examining clerks will read a letter of any length provided they find money enclosed in the letter to pay for it, at the rate of two and a half cents per page." In a four-page letter written to his mother, Thomas Morgan explained, "Many a time since my arrival here I determined to write and as often have deferred it until I could make 'small change' in order to write you a long letter." At least one Johnson's Island prisoner credited Gen. Merriwether Jeff Thompson with making the necessary arrangements for the system. Thompson, who drifted in and out of the Confederate Army during a colorful military career, later claimed that the deal earned the examiners an extra ten to twelve dollars a day. "But at last some mean 'cuss,' who had to pay ten cents for a four page letter, wrote to the commanding officer that he was taxed ten cents, and the matter was inquired into, and the long letter mail was suddenly stopped."[5]

On at least two occasions, the kindness of Union officials was as effective as bribery at getting the mail through. Before receiving the welcome letter from his sister, Ellis had gotten an empty envelope marked, "Letter contraband in length." The distraught Confederate appealed to Capt. John J. Manor. The next day he received his letter. "Captain Manor has my lasting thanks," Ellis wrote, "and if I ever catch him down South, I'll take care to remember that one 'Yankee' at least did me an act of kindness." Robert Bingham found himself in trouble after writing a private message to his wife and placing it under the stamp of a letter he sent her. It was, he explained in his diary, "just a word for her that I did not care for the Yanks seeing." He soon learned that other prisoners had used the same method to inform friends that there were secret messages in their letters, written with a "chemical ink" that would appear if placed over a flame. Bingham further discovered that camp officials had suspended his letters. He wrote to Pierson the same day, disavowing any intention of using chemical ink. The next day he received a note from the commandant informing him that his letters would be sent through. "The tone of the note was kind and courteous," the relieved captive wrote.[6]

Because of censorship, the letters of Civil War prisoners reveal little about life in the various camps. Instead, they demonstrate that the captives were constantly thinking of home. "I had hoped to eat my Christmas dinner at home," William G. Woods wrote in October 1864, "but I really expect to winter here again, unless something turns up—not expected now." In a letter written on December 3, 1863, Daniel S. Printup took advantage of information he had gained in the North to offer his family some advice. "Has Bro. P. sold my tobacco yet?" he asked. "If not, say to him not to be in a hurry. Tobacco crop in northern states was destroyed by frosts very bad, which will increase its price very much." Other letters contain a poignancy that requires no additional comment. "Please tell my sweetheart she may get married as soon as she likes," James Riddick wrote. "Release her from all obligations and hold her to the promise no longer as I expect never to get away from prison."[7]

Thoughts of home were especially strong on Sundays. "It is lonesome enough here every day in the week but Sundays seem more so to me than any other day," prisoner W. B. Gowen wrote one Sabbath. "Home and family have scarcely been absent from my mind to day." As they battled the loneliness of prison life, the captives often found comfort in their faith and determined to live more Godly lives. On his thirtieth birthday, John Joyes resolved to read one chapter of the Bible every day. "I have formed new rules for my future guidance," he noted, "and humbly ask of our Heavenly Father that at the experation of another ten years, if I shall be permitted to live so long, I can then say in every thing I have so lived as to make me worthy of a longer life." James Mayo experienced a similar epiphany. In a March 7, 1864, diary entry he announced, "After a serious reflection I sometimes think I do not give up enough for God." Mayo continued, "God help me to serve him aright for my own eternal salvation."[8]

Men of faith inevitably sought each other out, and prayer meetings and Bible studies became common events. William Peel noted that prisoners risked being shot so they could attend. "Notwithstanding the regulations which prohibit our passing from one Block to another, after dark, I see, at our nightly prayer meetings a good many faces that belong to neighboring Blocks," he wrote during a March 1864 revival. Peel obviously felt the results were worth the risk. "The cause of Christianity has made a triumphant march during the week. There have been a good many converts, & many others evince an interest in the Salvation of their Souls." According to Patterson, the daily prayer meetings were still going on in July. He wrote, "It does the soul good to hear the warm, earnest petitions that go up day after day and night after night, from the very depths of the hearts of the noble ones who linger here, to God, our Father, that he will have mercy on our bleeding country, and save her and our people."[9]

Except for the rule requiring the prisoners to remain in their blocks after dark, camp officials did nothing to interfere with the religious activities of the Confederates. On June 26, 1864, they paroled between thirty and forty prisoners, allowing them to go to the lake for a baptism ceremony. They also allowed religious tracts to be distributed to the captives, although Mayo complained that they were "much tainted with politics." In March 1864 the prisoners learned that a Union chaplain was to preach in Block 12. The announcement angered Patterson, who wrote, "I want no advice on religious matters from any one who at the same time is urging yankees to join in the attempt to subjugate us." Peel was more understanding, particularly after he learned that the chaplain had been invited by prisoners who had no pastor of their denomination. "Some gentlemen, who did not know of his having been asked to come in, supposed he was forcing himself on us," Peel noted, "& therefore declined to hear him &, I am sorry to say, treated him very disrespectfully, by both language & action, as he was leaving the yard."[10]

The scenery of the island itself occasionally offered a welcome diversion for the Confederate captives. In addition to the boats that passed in the summertime, the winter scenes proved compelling to many of the Southern natives. As December 1863 came to a close, Thomas Taylor observed, "The weather has been very pleasant and the ice on the lake, broken by the waves and drifted in piles upon the shoals and sandbars, presents a beautiful appearance in the rays of the morning sun." Even when not in freshets, the icy winter scenery impressed Virgil Murphey. "As far as the eye can extend," he wrote, "it is one unbroken sea of ice so brilliantly white when the sun is shining as to be painful to the Naked eye." However, the activities of Sandusky's civilians on the ice brought more mixed emotions. "The jingle of sleigh bells and the merry laugh of the sleighers as they perform innumerable gyrations on the pallid face of the ice comes like music to your ears and painfully remind you of captivity."[11]

James Mayo ventured out every evening to enjoy the music of the post band. His review was mixed. "It plays 'Coming Through the Rye' (much rye goes through to them) and one or two others that are quite pretty, but they have not a great variety of tunes." William Peel found the island to be a good spot for bird watching. On March 26, 1864, he observed "quite a flock of ducks" heading northward. By May 5 the bird population indicated that spring had definitely arrived. Peel observed, "Our black-birds are building all around; our woodpecker has been reinforced to double his original strength; & today a mocking-bird sang to us for a short time quite cheerfully."[12]

REBEL THESPIANS!

Acting and Stage Manager,_____Maj. GEO. McKNIGHT.
Treasurer,_____Lt. Col. J. C. HUMPHREYS.
Prompter,_____Capt. J. R. FELLOWS.
Scenic Artist._____Maj. SMITH.

☞ The management in the highest possible spirits, take great pleasure in stating that, at an enormous expense, a selection of the very finest dramatic talent known in the OLD and the NEW WORLDS has been made for the special delectation of the reinforcements strategetically sent to Johnson's Island by " Uncle Jeff." Every effort will be made by the management to astonish the natives in a most delightful manner. It is with feelings of pride that we point to the following

BRILLIANT ARRAY OF TALENT!

COL. BROWN, of Georgia,
MAJ. McKNIGHT, of Louisiana,
CAPT. CUSSONS, of Alabama.
CAPT. FELLOWS, of Arkansas.
CAPT. WASHINGTON, of North Carolina.
CAPT. YOUNGBLOOD, of Tennessee.
CAPT. McLOCHLAN, of Kentucky.
MAJ. COOK, of Mississippi.
LIEUT. HOUSTON, of Virginia.
LIEUT. PEELER, of Florida.

TOGETHER WITH

MISSES BROWN!
LAMAR!
COFFIN!
CANTRELL! and
STEWART!
AND A SUPERB CORPS DE BALLET !!!

Wednesday Evening, Oct. 7, 1863

THE STANDARD COMEDY OF

THE TOODLES!

FARMER ACORN,_____Capt. J. McLochlan.
GEO. ACORN, _____Lieut. T. D. Houston.
TIMOTHY TOODLES,_____Capt. J. W. Youngblood.
FARMER FENTON, _____Maj. Cook.
CHARLES FENTON,_____Maj. Bate.
LAWYER GLIB,_____Lieut. Dismukes.
1st. FARMER, _____Capt. Washington.
2nd. FARMER, _____Lieut. Lauchlin.
3rd. FARMER, _____Lieut. Long.
LANDLORD, _____Taylor.
MARY ACORN,_____Miss (Maj.) Stewart.
TABITHA TOODLES,_____Miss (Col.) Jack Brown.

SONG, - - - - - **Capt. E. F. Lamar.**

TO CONCLUDE WITH THE GREAT FARCE OF

SLASHER & CRASHER!

SLASHER,_____Maj. Geo. McKnight.
CRASHER,_____Capt. J. R. Fellows.
BLOWHARD,_____Capt. J. W. Youngblood.
CAPT. BROWN,_____Lieut. A. J. Peeler.
ROSA,_____Miss (Maj.) Stewart.
DINAH BLOWHARD,_____Lieut. Dismukes.

☞ In consequence of the immense expense attending the representation, the FREE LIST is ENTIRELY SUSPENDED!
☞ An Orchestra, expressly provided, at an immense expense of Butler's Checks, has arrived from Europe and other seaboard towns, and will entertain the appreciative audience with selections from the finest music ever heard on this or any other planet.
☞ The Sentinels on the outer walls have been specially engaged to preserve order and decorum.
☞ Little boys will not be allowed to eat pea nuts in the pit, nor throw orange peel from the gallery during the more affecting parts of the play. In order to carry out this arrangement more effectually, a special order will be issued, forbidding Joe Reynolds selling any of those articles to the little boys.

PRICES OF ADMISSION.

Dress Circle,_____Twenty-five Cents.
Parquette,_____Two Bits.
Pit,_____Two Dimes and a half.
Gallery _____Two Shillings.
Private Boxes,_____Quarter of a Dollar.
Reserved Seats, to be had only on Tuesday morning after 10 o'clock,_____Fifty Cents.

The Rebel Thespians printed this program for one of their performances. Such activities helped captives battle the boredom of prison life. (Courtesy Sandusky Library, Sandusky, Ohio)

A far different type of diversion occurred on September 2, 1864, when Johnson's Island witnessed its final execution. John J. Nickell was hanged after being found guilty by a court martial of the murder of two Union men in Kentucky and of being a guerrilla. Nickell admitted to killing the men, but he claimed that the pair had murdered his uncle and that he killed them in self-defense. Few prisoners mentioned the execution, which was carried out in a field west of the prison. One noted that the man's cousin, a prisoner at Johnson's Island, was allowed to visit him. Another expressed surprise at the large number of women present at the hanging.[13]

Despite these occasional diversions, prisoners at Johnson's Island had to depend on each other for virtually all of their amusement. Most often this came from ordinary social intercourse. In describing the captives' daily routine, J. L. Stockdale wrote that one of the most popular activities was "to visit the quarters of friends and acquaintances." The craze for autograph hunting came and went. "Such a getting of autographs I never saw," Mayo wrote in early 1865. "I have signed a great many today besides what I did some time ago." John Dooley's mess established a court, which assessed punishments for a variety of offenses. One prisoner who was found guilty "of some little misdemeanor," was "condemned by the court to fetch several buckets of water for the use of the room."[14]

"This being 'All Fools' day our boys had great sport in fooling one another," John Philip Thompson wrote on April 1, 1864. William Peel was more specific. Cooks were sent for rations that had not yet arrived, and proud Southern officers stared "with firy indignation," searching for non-existent black sentries. John Dooley was proud of a joke that seems to have bordered on the cruel. He secretly gathered up his messmates' old letters and persuaded a camp official to deliver them as if they had just arrived from the prisoners' loved ones.[15]

Perhaps the most frequent topic of conversation when captives gathered was the war. The Confederate officers were eager for any morsel of news, and rumors—known as "grape" in Civil War prisons—were common. Some were amazingly accurate. Two prisoners recorded the fall of Vicksburg on July 7, 1863, just three days after the Mississippi bastion surrendered. Both added that they and their comrades were skeptical and were awaiting further reports. On other occasions, the prison "grape" was far less reliable. On October 15, 1863, a prisoner reported that the rumor mill had Union Gen. George G. Meade, the victor at Gettysburg, replaced by Gen. Daniel Sickles, one of his corps commanders at that fight. Further, Sickles and General Lee were supposedly engaged in a battle at Manassas, Virginia.[16]

The most common topic of rumors was also the saddest. "For the 189th time we are all exchanged and will leave in a few days for Dixie," John Dooley wrote, revealing the frustration the stories produced. Another incarnation of the exchange rumor led William Peel to write, "Every body is spouting something about exchange. The yard is vocal with speculation on this subject." It was an observation that could have been made at one time or another in every prison on either side of the Mason-Dixon Line.[17]

Another common topic at all Union prisons was the election of 1864. Indeed, at least one prisoner at Elmira Prison in New York believed the prisoners were following the contest more closely than were their Union guards. The campaign pitted President Lincoln against Democratic challenger George B. McClellan, the general Lincoln had removed from command two years earlier. "There is a good deal of anxiety felt among us," William Peel wrote on election day. "We are generally in favor of McClellan, thinking his election will, at least, bring about an exchange of prisoners, & probably give us peace." After early returns indicated that Lincoln's reelection was likely, John Thompson "thought of the utter hopelessness of our release from prison [and] my heart almost sunk within me."[18]

The desire for news made newspapers a valuable commodity. "The newspapers are eagerly sought for and all the news items freely read and commented upon," one prisoner observed. He added, "The subject of an exchange of prisoners is the one that most deeply interests the men." For most of the war, the prisoners were allowed to purchase any newspaper they wanted, making Johnson's Island unique among Northern prisons. This changed on December 26, 1864, when "Peace Democrat" or "Copperhead" (depending on one's point of view) sheets were banned. One prisoner complained, "All the abolition newspapers strong and vehement in their advocacy of the war—of subjugation, of extermination, loyal support to the Administration and fierce and vindictive against rebels are permitted to enter when we pay the entrance fee."[19]

Books were also popular with the prisoners. All were allowed except texts on the subject of warfare. After receiving a shipment of reading material from a friend, John Porter wrote, "Our supply of books is now very respectable. Historical, Religious, Dramatic and Poetical." As the books arrived, the prisoners used their time—the only thing they had in abundance—to improve upon their education. "Quite a number of officers seem to have become, in a great measure, 'boys again,'" William Peel wrote as spring arrived in 1864. "Some of them have resumed the study of the languages, while many may be seen diligently employed with their slates, pencils, & Arithmetics or Algebries, & others are brooding over their grammars." Writing after the war, Col. B. L. Farinholt recalled that Johnson's Island had well-attended schools of law and medicine, and "a number of students, when released, entered upon useful and lucrative careers." The prisoners could also get mental stimulation by listening to lectures offered by their fellow captives. One, delivered by a Captain Griffith, was entitled "The Powers of Man, Physical, Moral and Intellectual."[20]

The "Island Prison Debating Society" considered a number of issues during the summer and fall of 1863. On one occasion the question was "Which exerts the greatest influence on men: money, wine or women." Women carried the day. When the prisoners considered "whether our imprisonment is beneficial or injurious to us," James Mayo termed it "hardly a debatable question." The debate topics sometimes took a political turn, discussing the potential policies of an independent Confederacy. One debate concerned the reopening of the African slave trade. Another topic was "Should the Confederate states recognize universal suffrage or a property qualification to entitle a citizen to vote?" Such discussions raised the ire of Union officials. Indeed, the latter debate was too much for the officer of the day, who broke up the gathering, announcing, in the words of one prisoner, that he "could not allow treason, and that the speeches of the parties were treasonable." The incident threatened to put a stop to the debates. Prison officials allowed them to continue, however, "if the crowd should not be too large, and if [the prisoners] would abstain from the great questions now at issue."[21]

A similar incident took place on February 22, 1864. The Yankees opened the morning with a celebration of Washington's birthday. Considering Washington to be "the Father of Rebels," the Confederates held their own impromptu ceremony. Their speaker was a Captain Fellows, who opened with a modest oration. After other speeches and a number from a prisoners' band, Fellows again stepped forward. This time he was considerably more political. As he delivered a line that began, "While the stars and stripes exultingly wave in the land of the thief & the home of knaves," the officer of the day showed up. Fellows was so enthusiastic that it took the blue-clad official a few tries to quiet him. He finally relented, and the ceremony was over. The celebrants returned to their blocks, although there were some hisses and a few cheers for Jeff Davis. According to Peel, the realization that the officer was only acting under orders prevented a serious incident. So too did "the recollection of a small 'Six pounder' we had often seen peeping through a loop hole at the upper end of the yard."[22]

A variety of groups offered less controversial entertainment to the Johnson's Island prisoners. "Went to a rehearsal of an operatic troupe and assisted on the flute and guitar," James Mayo wrote in the summer of 1863. It may have been the Island Minstrels, who gave a series of performances that year. Joseph Kern prepared a program for at least one performance. Working on it at one of the group's rehearsals, he observed, "Their music is quite creditable." The following summer saw the emergence of the "Rebelonians." William Peel described them as "a combination of negro minstrels & Thespian performance." A show Peel attended included "sentimental & comic songs," mostly written by the prisoners, "a number of ludicrous witticisms," a lecture, a banjo solo, and a play. "All seemed well pleased, except a couple of Yankees who were present, who didn't take a joke so well," Peel noted.[23]

During the fall of 1863, another group, the Thespians, attempted to offer entertainment that was more highbrow. According to John Dooley, a member of the group, "This new association wishes to improve on the Minstrels by abandoning the lees of wine or the glossy black of burnt corks and performing plays worthy of the intelligence and admiration of men of education and enlightenment." At least one critic felt that the group succeeded. After attending a performance of *The Battle of Gettysburg,* Robert Bingham wrote that it "was a really good play & the acting was very creditable to the Thespians." Success apparently went to the players' heads. They were soon demanding their own "dramatic hall," offering to build the structure themselves, and refusing to perform on extremely cold days. Block 12 offered a compromise, allowing them to erect a stage inside their barracks. Dooley even became critical of one of his fellow actors. "'Family Jars' is a complete success," he wrote, "but the 'Persecuted Dutchman' hops along on a lame leg. I fear our Dutchman has overdone his acting and in fact played himself out."[24]

Checkers, chess, and a variety of card games dominated indoor activities at Johnson's Island and other Union prisons. On April 19, 1864, William Peel observed that checkers "has been raging almost incessantly for several weeks past." While this may have been a temporary fad, games of chance were typically more popular. "The prisoners amuse themselves mostly by gambling," Robert Bingham noted. "Many play & many more look on." He added that it was not uncommon for a man to lose four or five hundred dollars in Confederate money in one day. Such proceedings disgusted Edmund Patterson. "Really the devil seems to be gaining ascendancy over the hearts of a large number confined here," he wrote in his diary. "Only a few nights since, while some of the more religiously inclined were holding prayer meeting, another party set up a Faro Bank and carried on the game all through the services in the same room, and not more than twenty feet from the meeting, and mingled their horrid oaths with the prayers as some unlucky turn would make them lose heavily."[25]

Warm weather brought the prisoners outside, and once again the opportunity to bathe in Lake Erie was one of the few bright spots of prison life. In 1864 a special order posted on the bulletin board in mid-June announced that the sessions were to be resumed. June 19 proved to be the first day. According to one diarist, every block got a turn that day, and "every one seems delighted with the refreshing influence of a good, cold bath." Indeed, as in 1862, the only complaint uttered by the prisoners concerned the appearance of voyeuristic women. "I saw something more of the depravity of the Yankee," Robert Bingham complained on July 9, 1863. "A good many she Yankee brutes came out and deliberately watched us." He was even more disgusted two days later when a group of women came to the rail of a passing boat and watched the men through opera glasses.[26]

According to John Dooley, another activity that was popular in 1862 also returned with a passion. "The prisoners nearly every evening are engaged in a game they call 'base-ball,' which notwithstanding the heat they prosecute with persevering energy," Dooley wrote during the 1864 season. He added, "I don't understand the game, but those who play it get very excited over it, and it appears to be very fine exercise." John Thompson played his first game on July 14, 1864, and was "very much pleased" with the pastime. Following his second game, Thompson wrote, "I think it an excellent game for exercise and the very thing I need to preserve good & perfect health." He may have reconsidered that assessment two weeks later after a bat slipped from a player's hands and struck a fellow prisoner in the forehead. The victim, a Captain Fellows, "threw both hands to his head, staggered & would have fallen to the ground, but he was caught by a gentleman near him. He lay quite insensible for several minutes." It was two days before a prison doctor announced that the captain's life was out of danger.[27]

On August 27, 1864, a game between the Confederate Club and the Southern Club "created more excitement than anything has done, in the yard, for a long time." The Southern team won 19–11. The contest lasted nine innings, and according to two prison diarists, wagers on the contest amounted to several hundred dollars.[28]

Lake Erie's harsh winters did not always put a stop to the prisoners' outdoor activities. During the bitter January of 1864, the Confederates at Johnson's Island engaged in at least three epic snowball fights. The contests pitted the upper six blocks against the lower six, and they lasted at least half a day. Participants pinned their block numbers to their hats so they could distinguish friend from foe. General Thompson commanded one army. He later recalled, "I was captured several times, and once nearly pulled in two by my friends trying to rescue me." Thompson added, "Sometimes after our battles the snow would be nearly as bloody as in actual conflict, for bloody noses and teeth knocked loose with snowballs were plentiful." At least one onlooker agreed, reporting, "Of course several got black eyes, bloody noses &c." Camp officials watched the battles, requesting copies of the after-action reports prepared by the participants.[29]

Although these activities went a long way toward alleviating the monotony of prison life, they did nothing about alleviating hunger, the prisoners' other constant companion. The captives realized that activities that promised a steady source of income were indispensable if they were to avoid "government rations." As Civil War prisons grew to the size of small cities—at least by the standards of the 1860s—they developed thriving business districts. The diversions in these prisons were many. But to the practical captive, the most important activities were those that not only allowed them to battle boredom but enabled them to fight hunger as well.

6

"A Matter of Necessity"

Prison Economics

Like any society, Civil War prisons housed a variety of social classes; and the officers confined at Johnson's Island were quick to assess the place of their fellow captives. "The society is of the very best to the lowest at your option," Thomas Gibbes Morgan informed his mother. In describing his messmates' visits to the sutler, Robert Bingham wrote, "We go down after the crowd is done & thus avoid being pushed & crammed by the rabble— and really many of the officers are the veriest rabble I ever saw."[1]

Although some officers liked to contend that it was their cultural attainments that set them apart from their fellows, financial means offered a more practical dividing line. "Our mess having plenty of money live as well in the way of eating as we ever did," John Dooley wrote. Thomas Taylor offered a cogent analysis of Johnson's Island society. "Those who are supplied with funds live very well," Taylor observed. "Hence, even in prison, where are a common cause and suffering, in common, can be seen that difference in society that is seen in other places, those who have ample means clinging together, with the usual number of toadies and dependents eagerly picking up the crumbs that their bounty lets fall to them."[2]

The "bounty" took various forms. For many prisoners, it came in the form of a box of provisions from home. The announcement of the arrival of such a box sent a wave of excitement through a mess. It brought with it the promise of clean clothing, books, cigars, and most important, delicacies not otherwise available. "I had the pleasure of receiving by express a couple of boxes which upon being opened proved to be filled with the greatest variety of niceties," William Peel wrote on March 31, 1864.

"An elegant ham, several pounds of sausage, quite a number of oranges & lemons & several pounds of sugar presented themselves in one, while the other contained quite a supply of chewing and smoking tobacco, a lot of candy, & several dozen new biscuits." On September 26, 1863, Robert Bingham was able to write, "I am Lucky about boxes now." One had arrived with clothing and handkerchiefs. Another contained peaches, tomatoes, and ketchup. A third prisoner informed a friend that he had dined with the mess of a colonel who had received some wine. He planned to eat with another mess that had been sent "a box of good things."[3]

For most of the war, Union officials placed few restrictions on boxes. Only such contraband items as uniform clothing, weapons, and hard liquor were excluded, and occasionally even the liquor found its way to the prisoners. The attitude produced a laissez-faire system that resulted in a strong sense of cultural Darwinism within the prison walls. Prisoners with the means were free to supplement their rations as they saw fit. All others had to do without. This stratified society was not limited to Johnson's Island. Fort Delaware prisoner Randolph Shotwell, whose postwar memoirs were harsh in their judgments about his Yankee guards, blamed his fellow Confederate captives for much of the suffering of his comrades. Many, he claimed, received all they wanted from boxes sent from home or purchases made at the sutler stand. Still, they refused to share even their prison rations with hungry comrades. Shotwell concluded, "It must be confessed that a portion of the officers were reprehensible in their thoughtlessness, or want of consideration, for the sufferings of their less fortunate circumstanced fellow prisoners."[4]

For prisoners with money, the sutler also offered a way to supplement government rations. In addition to eatables, the sutler offered tobacco, stationery, postage stamps, towels, glassware, and various personal care items. Prisoners spent according to their means, some discovering that by purchasing judiciously they could improve their fare for a low price. "At an expense of 8 or 10 cents a day," Robert Bingham wrote of his nine-member mess, "we have butter & molasses for breakfast & supper, & potatoes, onions &c for dinner."[5]

For most of the war, L. B. Johnson, owner of the island, acted as the prison sutler. He was less than a popular figure among the prisoners. Despite patronizing his stand and apparently appreciating the opportunity to improve upon his rations, Bingham termed Johnson "a most infamous lying, cheating scoundrel." The sutler earned the enmity of Bingham and other prisoners with a knack for creativity in cheating the Confederate captives. In January 1864 he offered photographs of the island for three dollars apiece. It was a souvenir that did not interest the prisoners, but Johnson informed them that if they did not purchase one, he would not sell them anything else. Eventually camp officials learned of the scheme. They not only put a stop to it but also made Johnson refund the purchase price.[6]

In March Johnson offered oil lamps for sale. They could be purchased along with a small quantity of lamp oil, and they sold well. The problem arose when the prisoners returned to replenish their supplies of oil only to learn that the Yankees had declared it contraband. Although the change in policy was not Johnson's fault, his refusal to take back the now worthless lamps for exchange understandably angered the prisoners. One was so upset that he struck the sutler in the head with his lamp. The blow shattered the lamp and felled Johnson. Before he could recover, the dissatisfied customer had fled the scene.[7]

To be able to make purchases from the sutler, the prisoners needed money. Some arrived well off in this regard. Others had relatives or friends in the North who were willing to send them the necessary funds. Those with neither money nor sources of obtaining it were forced to resort to their ingenuity. This proved to be virtually unlimited. All points along the social spectrum were represented. "There are many who with a laudable desire to earn money by the sweat of their brows, who by cooking, washing etc., manage to get enough of the circulating medium to obtain many comforts and conveniences," noted Thomas Taylor.[8]

From the professional ranks came one or more prison dentists who did not allow captivity to put a stop to their practices. "I suffered dreadfully last night with the tooth ache & went to one of our prison dentists & got him to commence working on them," John Thompson, wrote on May 17, 1864. By the time the dentist finished work the next day, Thompson had four teeth "plugged." He identified the doctor as a Captain Phillips. Seven months earlier John Dooley claimed that he helped launch the prison practice of "Lieut. Phillips of 10th Va. Cavalry." Dooley loaned money to the officer, enabling him to purchase the necessary supplies. In return the dentist promised to "plug and draw all my teeth free gratis, for nothing."[9]

Between dentists and day laborers on the economic scale came a number of skilled workmen plying a variety of trades. During the late summer months of 1864, chair making became a popular vocation. Some fashioned small lathes with which to work. Others used only pocket knives.

"The greatest difficulty is to get material for bottoms," one prisoner observed. "He who can get an old coffee sack is quite fortunate." The men took the sacks apart, straw by straw, and twisted the straws into cords. In his postwar reminiscences, Luther Rice Mills claimed that a group of enterprising prisoners used a concealed distillery to turn out "an inferior article of corn whiskey." Inferior or not, the brew fetched five dollars a quart. According to Mills, the still was so well hidden that it remained in place despite frequent inspections over a period of many months.[10]

On a July day in 1863, Joseph Kern strolled through Johnson's Island's business district, writing a description of some of the numerous enterprises:

> Passing up the street we see different signs displayed—Tailor Shop—Shoe Repairing—Beer & Cakes—Barber Shop—Pies—Green & Dried Apple Pies. One "Rebel" has opened a "Restaurant" with a regular "Bill of Fare." While passing along you can but note the apple vendors who stationed at regular intervals offer their apples to you. You will also meet boys with "Ice Cream & Lemonade." At nearly every kitchen biscuits [can] be had at 1 cent a piece. Apple Dumplings & sauce at 5 cents apiece.[11]

The most common vocation at perhaps every Union prison was the production of jewelry, buttons, and similar items. According to Thomas Taylor, Johnson's Island was no exception. "Nearly every mess has many workmen at this trade," he wrote, "and many articles of elegance and taste are manufactured." He added that "almost every man you meet has his fingers studded with rings and his bosom ornamented with a pin more or less richly set with gold, silver, or mother of pearl." Occasionally the prisoners purchased these items as gifts. "I sent on yesterday several beautiful Christmas presents to my dear little nieces," John Thompson wrote as the 1864 holiday drew near, "consisting of our Prison made jewelry." On another occasion a Johnson's Island captive sent his wife a ring he had bought from a fellow prisoner. In his letter, he conceded that it was likely too large, but he asked her to please wear it anyway.[12]

Most of the jewelry produced by the prisoners was sold outside the walls of the camps. As the historian Michael P. Gray discovered in researching his excellent study of the Elmira prison, Union guards and Confederate prisoners quickly learned that working together could be mutually profitable. The Yankees helped secure the needed raw materials to produce the jewelry and sold the finished products to eager customers on the outside. Sales were on a commission basis. The keepers in blue appear to have been honest in the transactions, and the system worked well for all parties concerned. At least one Elmira guard earned some five hundred dollars in just four months. He was so enthusiastic about the venture that he sent for a friend, who became his partner in the business.[13]

The prisoners employed many methods to secure the raw materials they needed. Some scoured their compounds for discarded bones and buttons. Friends on the outside kept others supplied with what they needed. High on the entrepreneurs' wish lists were pearl, gold, silver, and gutta percha, the substance resembling hard rubber obtained from the sap of tropical trees of the same name. Those whose other options were limited purchased what they needed and considered it among the costs of doing business. As at Fort Delaware and Point Lookout, Johnson's Island prisoners had the advantage of going to the beach. There they could find shells to ornament their products at no cost.

On February 4, 1864, William Peel entered the jewelry trade. He did not do so eagerly. "I regretted having it to do now but being without money it was a matter of necessity with me," he wrote. Three rings brought him a dollar and a half. Assisted by a friend, Peel also produced a couple of watch chains. When one sold for three dollars, he invested one-third of the money in enough material to make three or four more. On March 15 he offered an assortment of rings for sale. To his surprise, he sold a dozen, nearly all he had in stock, earning five dollars more. Despite his initial reluctance, Peel was soon enthusiastic about his prison enterprise. When he ran out of shell in early April, he was "getting into a fit of the blues on account of having nothing to do." A friend from Baltimore came to his rescue, sending a large supply of shell to the committed businessman. Two days after receiving it, Peel sold a cross he had fashioned from his new supply for $2.50. He also sent a pin, a watch chain, and a cross to his female benefactor. The busy jeweler still had enough material to maintain his business. May 8 proved to be one of his most profitable days. The sale, made to "a Yankee outside," consisted of a breast pin, nine studs, and a pair of sleeve buttons. Peel realized eight dollars from the transaction. The process repeated itself after another lot of shell arrived from Baltimore on May 17. After sending his supplier a pair of earrings, a bracelet, and a pin, he soon had a stock of goods ready to sell. On July 1 he sent a dozen breast pins, five collar buttons, and a number of other items to Baltimore, where he hoped his friend could sell them.[14]

Six days later Peel abruptly redirected his energies. "I have gotten somewhat tired of working in guttapercha," he announced in his diary, "& have turned my attention to making fans." In so doing, Peel went from one popular prison vocation to another. Indeed, fans appear to have been second only to jewelry in popularity among business-minded Confederate captives. Peel attacked his new venture with enthusiasm, and within two weeks he had completed twenty-seven fans. His plan was to ship them to his friend in Baltimore and another in Philadelphia to be sold for three dollars each. "Half this price will pay me very handsomely," he concluded.[15]

Seven days after sending out his initial shipment, Peel had another thirty fans ready to go. On August 25, eight weeks after abandoning the jewelry trade, Peel noted that he had made one hundred fans, sixty of which had gone to his distributors on the East Coast. He had sold a few in the prison for a dollar apiece and was holding the rest back to be "trimmed." It was November 23 before Peel next reported on his business dealings. His Baltimore friend informed him that she had sold twenty-six fans plus some jewelry that had been left over from earlier shipments. Peel's share of the proceeds amounted to sixty-four dollars. She sent him twenty-four and retained the rest to send him items he might later need. At that point, Peel, Johnson's Island's foremost diarist, had fewer than three months to live.[16]

If William Peel was among the most prolific businessmen at Johnson's Island, Lt. G. B. Smith, a Tennessee Confederate, was the most unique. When captured, Smith retained a photographic lens he was carrying. He installed it in a tobacco box and procured chemicals through the camp guards. The lieutenant set up his studio in the attic of his block. Customers had to climb a ladder and crawl across the rafters to reach a loose platform of boards that Smith had put in place. "Rebs in crowds visit him daily to have . . . their countenances faithfully delineated upon canvass," Virgil Murphey wrote. Murphey was among them. Although disappointed that Smith did not capture his entire beard, which reached to his waist, he felt that "the picture is otherwise very good." Murphey placed the price at one dollar. Another customer, John Dooley, wrote that the charge was fifty cents. He agreed with Murphey that the artist did excellent work on the photos, writing, "I am very well satisfied with mine."[17]

In 1864 Smith took a portrait of Robert C. Crouch, a fellow Tennesseean and Johnson's Island prisoner. Forty-five years later Crouch submitted the portrait to *Confederate Veteran,* a magazine largely composed of stories sent in by former Rebel soldiers. The picture ran in Volume 17 of the magazine. "Few artists would take a better picture now," the editors concluded.[18]

Smith may have had some competition from a different type of artist. In February 1864 John Thompson wrote in his diary that a Captain Cox had painted his portrait. Although Thompson noted that the captain was "a fine artist," no other Johnson's Island diarist mentioned him. It is not clear whether or not Cox charged for his work.[19]

To a large extent, Johnson's Island was an aberration among Civil War prisons. Virtually all of its captives were officers, meaning they came largely from the upper socioeconomic class of Southern society. This is not to say that the Sandusky depot was a pleasant place. Later in the war, after the Union instituted a policy of retaliation, it became even less so. Still, through 1863 and much of 1864, Johnson's Island prisoners had an advantage over their comrades in other camps when it came to battling the boredom and the hunger that came with prison life.

7

"A Guard for Unarmed Men"

Guards and Commanders

Despite any misgivings William Hoffman harbored concerning his young protégé, William Pierson remained in command at Johnson's Island as the prison population swelled after the collapse of the exchange cartel. On August 25, 1863, he received a promotion to lieutenant colonel. A short time later, however, circumstances changed, forcing the commissary general to reexamine the command structure at the Lake Erie prison. The Union was seriously considering a policy of retaliation because of the treatment of Union prisoners held in the South. On November 11 Hoffman suggested to the War Department that the Hoffman Battalion be increased to regimental strength. He further recommended that "the whole be placed under the command of an energetic and reliable officer of senior rank to the present commander." In a letter to Governor Tod, Hoffman was more blunt. "I do not know whether you are at liberty to select a Colonel for the regiment," he wrote, "but if it is in your discretion to do so, I would respectfully recommend that you select some energetic and reliable soldier for the position, if you can find such a one available." Hoffman explained, "Col. Pierson is very attentive to his duties and very kind and courteous in his manners, but he has not sufficient force to meet the responsibilities of such a command."[1]

On January 13, 1864, the 1st Brigade, 3rd Division, 6th Army Corps, five regiments strong, arrived at Sandusky. The next day Brig. Gen. Henry D. Terry, commander of the brigade, assumed command of the Post of Sandusky and of Johnson's Island. The 65th and 67th New York and the 23rd and 82nd Pennsylvania Infantries were stationed on the island. The 122nd

New York, along with Terry, remained in Sandusky. Pierson continued his daily duties at the prison, subject to Terry's orders. He remained until July 15, when he resigned his commission.[2]

On January 19 Hoffman informed the new commander that the Hoffman Battalion had been brought up to regimental strength. The newly christened 128th Ohio Volunteer Infantry was on its way to Johnson's Island. Col. Charles W. Hill was the commander of the regiment. "I respectfully suggest," Hoffman wrote Terry, "that he with his regiment be placed in immediate charge of the depot, making it a command distinct from your brigade." The commissary general also called Terry's attention to a recent medical inspection and its report that "the police of the prison is in a very unsatisfactory condition." He asked that the general issue whatever orders were necessary to improve the situation.[3]

If Hoffman hoped that Terry as the new commander would produce positive changes at the prison, the commissary general apparently did not get his wish. In early May Lt. Col. John F. Marsh submitted a damning inspection report to Col. James A. Hardie, inspector general of the U.S. Army. "But little judgment is exercised in the management and discipline of the prison," Marsh wrote. He found the grounds and barracks of both the garrison and the prison poorly policed. The sinks were "offensive," so much so that the inspector feared for the health of the post as warmer weather approached. The wood supplied to the prisoners, Marsh reported, was of poor quality and overpriced. L. B. Johnson, owner of the island, had supplied it, and the inspector stopped just short of accusing him and Pierson of collusion in the matter. He observed that the former commander "appears greatly interested in Johnson's affairs." As for the current commander, "General Terry is an intelligent, clever gentleman, but quite as fond of a social glass of whisky as of attending to the duties of his command."[4]

On May 9, 1864, Hill and the 128th arrived at Johnson's Island. The unit replaced the 82nd Pennsylvania Infantry, which had been stationed there for just two weeks. Col. Isaac C. Bassett, the unit's commander, had been in command of the prison during that time. Hill succeeded both Bassett and Terry, assuming command of United States forces both on the island and at Sandusky. He would remain for the remainder of the war.[5]

As he had with Terry, Hoffman tried to impress upon Hill the need for reforms at the prison he had created. He wrote to the new commander on May 29, calling his attention to letters he had previously sent to both

Col. Charles W. Hill assumed
command of the prison in May
1864. (Courtesy Massachusetts
MOLLUS Collection, United
States Army Military History
Institute, Carlisle Barracks, Pa.)

Pierson and Terry. "I request you will at once put all the desired reforms
in force," Hoffman urged. These included cleaning up the sinks, which he
termed a "nuisance," and improving the policing of the camp.[6]

Unlike his predecessors, the energetic Hill required no prodding from
above. The new commander soon issued a flurry of general orders, address-
ing a variety of problems. He ordered weekly inspections of the guard force.
The daily prison guard was to consist of a captain as officer of the day, a
lieutenant as officer of the guard, 3 sergeants, 8 corporals, and 102 privates.
To combat drunkenness, Hill issued orders forbidding men leaving on pass
or furlough to take their canteens with them. Few details escaped the vigilance of the energetic colonel. Hill even regulated the schedule of the ferry
between Sandusky and the island "in order to provide better facilities for
transporting supplies to this island with sufficient opportunity to load and
unload." When the post band went to Port Clinton to play a concert, their
leader was warned that if any members "get drunk or otherwise misbehave
themselves no further excursions of the kind will be permitted."[7]

On August 6, 1864, Maj. Edward Scovill of the 128th was promoted to lieutenant colonel. By that time Scovill was already serving as superintendent of prisons. In that position he was largely responsible for the day-to-day operations of the depot. He also conducted the weekly prison inspections, which Hoffman began requiring at all posts in the spring of 1864. Forty years after the war, one former prisoner remembered Scovill as a considerate officer. James F. Crocker, who was captured at Gettysburg, recalled that he had wished to write letters longer than were allowed to a girl back home. Scovill told the Rebel to hand the letters to him personally and he would get them through. "That kind act of Colonel Scovill made him my personal friend," Crocker wrote, "and afterwards he did me other important kindnesses."[8]

The prisoners' opinion of Colonel Hill was mixed. John Joyes was one Confederate who held the commandant in high esteem. "The commander of this post . . . certainly, according to the transactions which I have had with him, seems to act with uniform courtesy, and in a just and considerate manner while carrying out strictly his orders from Washington," Joyes wrote late in the war. Others felt differently. In June the commandant posted an order declaring that entire blocks would be held responsible for the actions of individual prisoners. If members of a block attempted to tunnel out of the prison, their comrades were required to report them. If they failed to do so, rations would be withheld for the entire block. "He has thus made a sentinel of each prisoner," William Peel wrote. Peel added a prison rumor that Hill had made a "dashing charge . . . in the wrong direction" at the Battle of Cheat Mountain early in the war. Edmund Patterson had apparently heard the same rumor. Responding to the order that so infuriated Peel, he wrote, "It would give any of us much more pleasure to cut his throat than to make any kind of report to him, though so base a coward as he has proven himself to be (in Virginia) does not deserve an honorable death."[9]

The prisoners held Hill's regiment in similar contempt. In describing the outfit before it was brought up to regimental strength, Joseph Kern wrote, "The battalion is rather small; are Sunday soldiers; at least present that appearance when compared with the old soldiers of the field. Their fine dress uniforms, brass epaulets, Kossuth hat, with plume, and regulation cord and tassel, white gloves, and blackened boots. No field duty expected with their enlistment; a guard for unarmed men." It was an opinion commonly expressed among Civil War prisoners, who held no respect for guards who had not seen service at the fighting front. When the guards from the Sixth

Corps departed in the spring of 1864, Peel was sorry to see them go. "The news excites a good deal of regret among us since we will then be left again to the Hoffman Battalion, who have never been in the field, & whom we have consequently not had an opportunity of teaching respect to us."

R. D. Chapman held a similar view of the Johnson's Island keepers. Chapman arrived at the prison in September 1863. He remained for five months before escaping from a train while being transferred to Fort Delaware. Upon reaching his home in Georgia, Chapman wrote in the *Macon Telegraph* that his fellow prisoners at Johnson's Island "were subjected to great insults and abusive language by the guard, which was composed of the most vulgar and degraded characters, who volunteered to guard prisoners and refused to meet them on the battlefield." Ironically, Chapman's next assignment was as an adjutant at Camp Sumter, the infamous Georgia prison camp known better as Andersonville.[10]

If records of courts-martial are any indication, the men of the 128th appear to have caused their officers as much trouble as they did the prisoners. Eight men were tried at an August 5, 1864, proceeding. Four were found guilty of being absent without leave. Two others pronounced guilty had been absent from guard duty. A sergeant was found guilty of conduct prejudicial to good order and military discipline. He had been caught gambling with cards with three privates and had later refused to remove his hat at the breakfast table. On October 25 twelve more men were found guilty of being absent without leave. The same offense produced thirty convictions at a December 1 proceeding, and ten more were found guilty just five days later. Others were convicted of conduct prejudicial to good order and military discipline. Specifications included making noise after being ordered not to, missing roll call, conversing with prisoners, and refusing an order to cut wood.[11]

As winter approached and ice began to cover the lake, it became easier for the men—at least those up to a bracing walk—to absent themselves from the camp. Hill addressed the problem with a pair of orders. One required four roll calls a day "to detect and bring to proper accountability men who go away from the post without permission." Offenders were threatened with time in the guardhouse, being placed in irons, and extra police work. The second order required officers to collect passes when men under their command returned.[12]

Hill was no easier on subordinates or contractors who cheated prisoners. On August 22, 1864, he complained to the commissary of subsistence at Sandusky, "I have it on reliable authority that your subordinates issue necks, shanks, hearts and livers quite generally to prisoners." He added, "The beef ration for prisoners is 14 ounces, and I suppose those 14 ounces must consist of "beef" according to regulations." On December 3 Hill directed his wrath at a private contractor in Sandusky. "The quality of the lot of fresh beef yesterday inspected and ordered to be thrown back on your hands was disgraceful to you," he wrote, "and it will not be condusive to your interest to repeat the experiment."[13]

Hill could be equally brusque in dealing with matters of prison discipline. After prisoners removed a table from the mess hall, the colonel ordered Scovill to "use every exertion to find out who the men are that committed the depredations." If discovered, the guilty parties were to be placed in close confinement and on half rations for two days. If not, the entire block where the lumber from the table was found was to go on half rations for the same period. "The prison regulations must be strictly enforced," Hill demanded.[14]

Punishments varied from prison to prison. Hoffman seldom interfered with his commandants' disciplinary policies except in the most extreme cases. "Riding the mule" was a frequent punishment at some camps, particularly Camp Douglas. Prisoners were made to sit on the sharp edge of a board that had been placed on a platform. They were often required to remain there for several hours. Elmira prisoners who violated the rules often found themselves wearing a "barrel shirt," an open-ended barrel that rested heavily upon their shoulders. A placard naming the man's offense was often attached. "Bucking and gagging" was a particularly cruel punishment. It involved placing a block of wood in the prisoner's mouth and holding it in place with a cord bound tightly to the back of the head. Although many postwar memoirs talk of prisoners being hung by their thumbs, contemporary diarists mention it very rarely. A more common form of punishment was the ball and chain. It was not unusual at most camps to see prisoners who had violated one rule or another dragging around sixteen- to thirty-two-pound balls.[15]

For the officers held at Johnson's Island, time in close confinement was a dreaded punishment. "The fate of the other prisoners is paradise compared to their situation," Thomas Taylor wrote. The offenders had a small yard for exercise during the daytime, but they spent their nights in one of two small, windowless huts. According to William Peel, summer nights in the unventilated cabins had to be excruciating. "I can scarcely see how the poor fellows escape suffocation," he wrote on June 27, 1864, "for the heat is such that I can hardly live on my cot in the middle of a large room, with four windows & two doors open." The confinement area, located in the southeastern section of the camp, was kept isolated from all other prisoners, who had strict orders to keep away. All of the men kept there were in irons, with a thirty-two-pound solid shot attached. In September 1864 both sides agreed to release all prisoners held in irons, and close confinement at Johnson's Island came to an end. As the prisoners emerged from their punishment, Peel wrote, "I imagine [even] with all their present restrictions, they feel, by contrast, almost that they have been turned loose into the world again."[16]

At virtually every Civil War prison, the captives knew the penalty for stepping across the aptly named "dead line." It was generally located some twenty feet from the wall, and it marked the boundary of how close to that wall any prisoner could approach. Although the guards would occasionally shout out a warning before firing upon men who crossed it, this was not always the case. At Camp Douglas a railing about eighteen inches high served as the dead line. At other camps a ditch sufficed. Johnson's Island's dead line was marked by a row of stakes.[17]

Most shootings at Union prisons did not involve dead-line infractions. More often shots were fired at prisoners for being out of their barracks after dark. Guards also fired frequently into barracks in which prisoners burned lights after dark, which rules prohibited at all prisons. As he did with punishments, Hoffman generally allowed camp commanders to handle shooting incidents as they saw fit. This changed in 1864, following four separate occurrences at Camp Chase. In one case a prisoner who was shot by a guard in the middle of the night did not receive medical attention until late the next morning, a situation Hoffman termed "barbarous and without possible excuse." On March 17 the commissary general ordered that a board of officers investigate all shootings and report the results to him. These boards tended to exonerate the guards in question, with at least one notable exception. A guard at Camp Morton, near Indianapolis, had "repeatedly threatened to 'shoot some rebel,' stating that they had shot two fingers off for him . . . while he was in the field." He made good on his threat, killing a prisoner from Mississippi. The camp commander ruled that the shooting was "a malicious and premeditated act," and ordered murder charges be filed. The outcome is not known.[18]

Shooting incidents were less common at Johnson's Island than at other Union prisons. However, they were certainly not unheard of. As far as the prisoners were concerned, the incidents were often unjustified. "The Yankees are getting quite bold," Robert Bingham wrote on January 16, 1864. "They know they are too strong for us now & these infamous home guards, Hoffman's Bat., are getting large & shooting at everybody—shot several times last night." One of the intended victims was a man who left his block to use the sinks, which the prisoners were allowed to do. The sentry fired without warning. Fortunately his marksmanship was no better than his judgment. Six months later, according to prisoner John Washington Inzer, the guards were again getting bold. "The yankees here guarding us have been keeping up a regular fire on us a large portion of the time," Inzer wrote on July 24. "Last night, two officers in Block 5 . . . were seriously wounded. Such shameful cowards the yankees are," he concluded. [19]

Occasionally the prison diarists conceded that the guards were justified in firing at prisoners. "One of the prisoners was shot at by a Sentinel early this morning," W. B. Gowen wrote on June 29, 1863. The man had left his block and started across a street before reveille, which Gowen noted was a violation of the prison rules. The guard ordered the man to halt before firing, but he ignored the warning. Once again, the shot did not find its mark. [20]

The guards fired a number of shots on the night of July 15–16, 1864. Edmund Patterson and William Peel both suspected that the Yankees had heard rumors of a plot to release the prisoners. According to Patterson, a squad of guards came into the yard, fired shots into four different blocks, and shouted out the order that any man who stepped out the door of his barracks that night would be shot. Peel confirmed Patterson's account of the order, but he did not believe the shots were fired randomly. Rather, his information indicated that the shots had all been fired at Block 13, where at least one man was loitering just outside the block. Whatever the cause, no one was injured. [21]

One week later, Peel wrote in his journal that a shot had been fired into Block 5 the previous night. According to Patterson, who was quartered in Block 5, a sentinel had ordered the lights in the block extinguished. The prisoners attempted to explain that there were no lights burning. What he was seeing was a reflected light from the window of the nearby hospital. The sentinel did not believe the claim and fired. The ball passed through one man's arm, shattering the bone below the elbow, before lodging in another man's shoulder. Hill promised that the guard would be punished, but Patterson was skeptical. "This is the fifth time they shot into the blocks," he wrote, "but fortunately heretofore their shots have been harmless."[22]

Indeed, if the prisoners' diaries can be believed, the guards at Johnson's Island often posed a greater threat to prison property and personnel than they did to miscreant captives. On June 12, 1864, Peel wrote that a shot had rung out the previous night at about the time for "lights out." The victim of the shooting turned out to be an old barrel that the sentinel had "converted into a Reb's appearance." Six months earlier a potentially more serious incident had occurred. According to Patterson's diary, during the night of December 12–13, 1863, a guard "shot an adventurous yank who was prowling about during the night, probably trying to steal something." Patterson added, ungenerously, "Unfortunately however, he was only wounded, and it is feared that it will not prove fatal."[23]

The main job of the Johnson's Island sentinels, of course, was to keep their Confederate captives on the island; and despite their occasional lapses in judgment, the men of the 128th performed their duty well. The Lake Erie depot proved to be one of the most difficult Union prisons from which to escape. This did not keep the resourceful Rebels from trying, however, and their attempts—successful or not—make for some of Johnson's Island's most exciting tales.

8

"Almost a Fixed Impossibility"

Escapes and Attempts

In July 1862 all Union prison camps began forwarding monthly returns to Colonel Hoffman. According to the reports sent from Johnson's Island, only twelve Confederate prisoners escaped from the Lake Erie depot between then and the end of the war. Even if these figures can be questioned, it is beyond doubt that the prison was among the most secure of Union facilities, the Alcatraz of the North. Those fortunate enough to make it beyond the walls of the camp faced a daunting swim in the summertime or bitter cold and winds in the winter. Anyone overcoming all these obstacles would then be confronted with a lengthy trek through hostile territory.[1]

Camp officials used numerous tools to prevent potential escapes, starting with what former prisoner B. L. Farinholt referred to as "many large reflecting lamps posted around within the prison." Virgil Murphey wrote, "Escape, liberation from these blank walls is almost a fixed impossibility." He explained, "The palisades are tall and perpendicular and [there is] no cover nor protection to advance upon them. Huge lanterns suspended from them throws a flood of light over the entire enclosure and thus you are robbed of the friendly cover of night."[2]

The greatest threat to the escapees' plans often came from their fellow prisoners. At Johnson's Island, as well as other camps, captives who were either planning to take the oath of allegiance or simply eager for extra rations would often betray their fellow captives. Dubbed "razorbacks" by the other prisoners, one of them received the blame when the guards foiled an escape attempt on the night of June 2, 1864. A group of prisoners had spent several weeks digging a tunnel from the "dead house," the building where coffins were kept and bodies were taken to be prepard for burial. The work was complete, and the freedom-bound Rebels were only waiting for dark when the guards arrived. "They came straight to the spot without waiting to look around at all," Edmund Patterson wrote. "Some spy had told them all about it." In January 1865, the Union guards stopped another group of would-be escapees who were attempting to tunnel out of camp. The federal officer told the leader of the party that his efforts were futile because the Yanks knew about the project within a half hour after it was begun. He proved his point by giving the exact time that the prisoners had started digging. "They are kept perfectly posted on all these points," William Peel observed, "and it seems impossible for us to catch their spies."[3]

Frequent surprise inspections, likely prompted by information supplied by the razorbacks, may have also helped thwart a number of escapes. Improvised ladders were a common target of these searches, but the guards often extended them to include personal items. "I could not help thinking that in a carpet sack or letter box was a rather strange place to look for a ladder," one prisoner noted after a Sunday morning inspection. The guards also searched for surplus clothing, which the prisoners were not allowed to have. When word of an impending search reached the prisoners, they made certain to wear the best clothing they had, risking the rest. "Our Block made, perhaps, the most genteel appearance at roll-call, this morning that they ever have for a long time," Peel wrote following a report that an inspection was about to be conducted. "Every man turned out in the best he had, & in a full suit, too, if he had it."[4]

Officially, there were no escapes at Johnson's Island during 1863. However, according to prison diarist John Dooley, the official returns were not correct. On October 1 Dooley recorded that a group of prisoners had been quickly recaptured after crawling through a hole they had cut in the fence. In noting the incident, he added that the camp had seen only one successful escape. It occurred when a prisoner hid under some straw in a supply boat that serviced the island. He knew the man made it back to Dixie, Dooley continued, because "his friends in the prison have heard from him."[5]

On November 3 W. B. Gowen and Robert Bingham described a failed attempt to tunnel out of the camp the previous night. Both agreed that five men made it through the tunnel, while a sixth became trapped when the chamber at least partially collapsed. According to Bingham, the man cried out in desperation, betraying the escapees. Both agreed that he was close to death when rescued by the guards. "They have all been kept at work today digging a ditch between the House [Block 1] & Wall to prevent any more tunneling in that quarter," Gowen wrote.[6]

Cold weather foiled the next escape attempt. A Captain Boyd, who resided in Block 11, selected the night of January 1, 1864, to make the effort. It was a bad choice, as the temperature plummeted to well below zero. He managed to evade the guard but the bitter weather forced him to return. Camp officials, apparently feeling that he had learned his lesson, permitted him to return to his block. Once back in the room, Boyd informed his messmates that the cold had lessened the vigilance of the sentries. Anyone who could get sufficient warm clothing, the captain suggested, might stand a good chance of making it to freedom.

Boyd's report inspired five of his fellow prisoners, who decided immediately to make the attempt. They procured extra clothing from their comrades and quickly improvised a ladder. A sixth captive, Lt. Thomas White, volunteered to hold the ladder for them and sneak it back to the block so the escape would not be discovered. All five men managed to scale the wall, but the last one over made some noise, attracting the attention of the nearest sentinel. To distract him, White rushed back to the block, banging the ladder against the building for effect. The guard, believing he had thwarted an escape attempt, and likely not eager to leave the shelter of his sentry box, remained at his post.

The next morning other prisoners answered at roll call for the escapees. By this time, the prisoners were inspired by the success of their comrades, and several decided to make the try themselves. That night, in the words of one prison diarist, "The drains and ditches were at times crowded with men creeping towards the fence to escape." It was too late. The cold had abated somewhat, the guards were more alert, and every attempt was greeted with shots from the sentry boxes. One prisoner got away temporarily by knocking a sentinel from the wall with a piece of wood, but he was recaptured and placed in irons. Also returning to the prison on January 3 was one of the five men who had escaped two nights before. It was the last man to clear the fence, the prisoner who made the noise that alerted the sentinel. He had hidden in the bushes, becoming separated from his comrades. Half frozen by the time he reached the mainland, the prisoner had taken refuge with a farmer, claiming to be an unemployed sailor. His tale deceived the farmer, who took him to a nearby train station the next day. There he encountered a detective who was less easily fooled.

According to the official January return from Johnson's Island, three prisoners successfully escaped. The occupants of Block 11 got official confirmation from at least one of them. And as the month ended, they received a letter from one of the five who made the original attempt. It was postmarked Montreal. Eight years later, one of the escapees told his story to *Southern Magazine*. The four men had made their way to the mainland and pushed on through the bitter night. Shortly before sunrise they stopped at a farmhouse for warmth and breakfast, claiming to be land speculators. They then resumed their journey but had to leave behind one member of their party who grew too ill to continue and was later recaptured. The remaining trio headed north into Michigan, crossing the wide Detroit River into Ontario and safety.[7]

Although the February 1864 return indicated that no prisoners escaped, two Johnson's Island diarists wrote of a successful escape on the 20th. According to William Peel, a Confederate captain in a blue overcoat went through the gates when a few prisoners were allowed out to fetch water from the lake. He pretended to buy some trinkets made by the prisoners before continuing on his way. James Mayo recorded the same basic story with the exception that he claimed more than one Rebel employed the ruse to begin his journey to freedom. It is possible that the man or men were recaptured, but neither Peel nor Mayo ever indicated so. Peel did report that a number of prisoners tried the same tactic the next day. Their numbers, however, betrayed them. The following month a prisoner, "putting on his best Yankee looks," was passed out of camp by a sentry. Unfortunately the ice was too thin to allow him to cross, and he was forced to return to camp.[8]

On August 8, 1864, Colonel Hill received a "confidential note from a prisoner vaguely cautioning me that a plot was on hand requiring my immediate attention." The commandant ordered the guard increased and had a patrol of eighty men standing by to conduct a search if necessary. He also questioned the sentinels at the gates, discovering that one had allowed several men to pass out. Hill dispatched his patrol to scour the island. They found eighteen Confederates. All were wearing regulation blue trousers and shirts that were similar to Union uniforms. A search of the blocks produced several more articles of blue clothing, and a subsequent roll call revealed that two prisoners were missing. Once again, their fellow prisoners had answered for them at the intervening roll calls.[9]

According to Edmund Patterson, the first escapee had secured a shovel and passed out with a work party on the evening of August 6. As with the

The Hoffman Battalion, later the 128th Ohio Volunteer Infantry, served as the primary guard force at Johnson's Island. (Courtesy Sandusky Library, Sandusky, Ohio)

previous attempts, his success inspired imitators. The next day, William Peel wrote, the men saw another opportunity. The Yankees were hauling lumber into the camp in wagons. The Confederates put on their blue outfits and either followed the wagons out or jumped in for a ride.

"The game of going out was resumed this morning in good earnest," Peel observed on the 8th. "Every body that could raise a Yankee suit was trying the trick." Both he and Patterson agreed that each wagon that passed out contained half a dozen prisoners. Diarist John Washington Inzer placed the total number at fourteen. The scheme abruptly ended when a prisoner, lacking the proper uniform, "tried the trick" in a red shirt. The sentinel challenged him. When he asked the man, who insisted that he was a Union soldier, to identify his company, the prisoner hesitated. "This was enough to excite suspicion," Peel wrote. This, he added, prompted the search of the island, contradicting Hill's report to Hoffman of an anonymous note. It was further contradicted by one of the escapees who was later apprehended, who told Peel the commandant had interrogated him. "He told me if the boys had stopped when ten or a dozen had gone out, that number might have escaped, as his suspicions were not excited, until the man in the red shirt was caught."[10]

Two days after the red-shirted Confederate ruined his comrades' dreams of liberty, a captain from South Carolina attempted a similar scheme. A new group of men was working at the sutler's stand, and the guards had not yet become familiar with all of them. The captain, dressed in civilian clothing similar to theirs, was passed through the gate, but his luck ran out as he boarded the ferry to Sandusky. A Union sergeant recognized him and returned him to the camp.[11]

The next escape from Johnson's Island did not find its way into any prison diaries, but it was mentioned by Lieutenant Colonel Scovill in his weekly inspection report submitted on September 18, 1864. Lt. J. G. Odom, a North Carolina officer, had absconded. "There is no definite knowledge as to the manner [of escape]," the prison superintendent conceded, "but it is presumed he personated one of the roll-callers and eluded the vigilance of the gate keeper." In forwarding the report, Hill distanced himself from any possible responsibility for the escape. He informed Hoffman that the soldier responsible for calling the roll had failed to follow his instructions, although he did not specify what those instructions were. To drive the point home, Hill concluded, "The roll-callers are directly under the command of the superintendent of the prison and he is responsible for the disregard of instructions."[12]

On the night of October 4, 1864, Capt. Robert C. Kennedy of the First Georgia Infantry escaped by scaling the wall and apparently made his way to the mainland on a small skiff. Maj. Thomas Linnell, who temporarily succeeded Scovill, placed the blame on the roll callers. This time, however, Hill disagreed. The commandant reported to Hoffman that a prisoner named Smith had inadvertently been removed from the rolls. Not having to answer to his own name, he had answered for Kennedy, concealing the escape.[13]

On the night of December 12–13, 1864, a group of twenty-five to thirty prisoners charged the wall, armed with about ten improvised ladders, in a desperate attempt to escape. The first volley from the guards chased most of the party back. Among those who pressed forward was Lt. John B. Bowles, a Kentucky prisoner. He was hit twice and died instantly. His death was doubly tragic, because his father, a Confederate lieutenant colonel, was also a Johnson's Island prisoner. According to a guard with the 128th Ohio Infantry, two other prisoners were wounded. Six made it across the fence, but the conditions they then encountered made escape nearly impossible. The moon was bright, and the snow that covered the ground reflected its light. Their route was across open fields, providing no place to hide. In addition, area farmers, hearing blasts of artillery from the island, soon had every road guarded.[14]

All of the escapees were quickly brought back to the camp except one. A Lieutenant Caruthers had scaled the fence bare-handed and had neglected to put his gloves on until he reached the mainland. With his hands "perfectly numb and useless," he lay down to rest. This worked to his advantage, as the guards passed him in their pursuit of the others. After recovering somewhat, the lieutenant continued through the darkness. At about daylight, after going some seven or eight miles, he could continue on no farther. He spotted a farmhouse and decided "to risk the chances" by seeking help. The farmer met him at the gate and immediately realized who he was. "I don't wish to arrest you, but I can't give you shelter," the farmer said. The desperate Caruthers surrendered to the farmer, trading the hope of freedom for warm shelter. That afternoon the citizen returned him to the authorities.[15]

Three escapes between December 24, 1864, and January 5, 1865, led Colonel Hill to conclude that prisoners were passing out through the gate in Union uniforms. On the morning of Christmas Eve, Capt. Robert McKibbin escaped. It was twenty-four hours before guards realized he was gone. On January 2 Col. Daniel R. Hundley of the 31st Alabama Infantry escaped just after the morning roll call. Once again, it was a full day before his absence was known. Three days later, Lt. Rufus Jones of the 9th Alabama made his way out of camp, apparently passing out with the roll callers. "He is supposed to have been in the uniform worn by our soldiers," Hill reported, "including the fatigue cap and light blue overcoat." This caused the colonel to question the assertion of a number of prisoners that McKibbin had escaped from a watering party and Hundley from a burial detail.

Hill sent Jones's description out to the press and offered a reward of a hundred dollars for his recapture. He also relieved the gatekeeper from duty. Jones got away, but the reward Hill posted resulted in the capture of Hundley. He was arrested by a citizen of nearby Fremont, Ohio, who assumed that he was Jones.[16]

On January 22 a Lieutenant Goss of North Carolina tried the same tactic. He was detected and given the choice of being sent to close confinement or standing on the head of a barrel in the cold for five hours. He chose the latter. According to Virgil Murphey, the punishment did not sit well with the prisoners, who felt it was the right of a prisoner to attempt to escape. "Col. Hill endeavored to explain away in an order this open and vindictive violation of a principle universally acknowledged but failed and increased the indignation of the pen," Murphey wrote. Inzer agreed. Terming the punishment "an awful outrage," he added, "Hill ought to be hung by the heels for this vile act." When the colonel repeated the punishment for another would-be escapee six days later, Inzer wrote, "Mean act. Hill is a fiend."[17]

No Johnson's Island prisoner was more persistent—or more resourceful—in his attempts to escape than Lt. Charles Pierce of the 7th Louisiana Infantry. Although he never succeeded in getting away from the prison, his attempts have made him the stuff of legends. Despite being residents of Cincinnati, "Charlie" Pierce and two brothers cast their lot with the Confederacy when the war broke out. Their family had long been in the shipping business, and their numerous trips to New Orleans likely influenced the Pierces' decision. So too may have relatives residing in Kentucky. In November 1863 Charlie Pierce was among a number of Confederates scooped up by Unionists while guarding a bridge on the north bank of the Rappahannock River in Virginia. The captives were taken to the Old Capitol Prison in Washington, D.C., but Pierce and the other officers were soon transferred to Johnson's Island.[18]

Pierce was a member of the party that scaled the wall on the night of December 12–13, 1864. He was also among those returned by civilians. For Pierce, the failed escape was especially sad. Lieutenant Bowles, the man fatally shot in the attempt, was his cousin. The next month he joined a group planning to tunnel out of camp. This proved to be the party betrayed by a razorback who had told the guard the exact time they had started to dig.

At this point Pierce decided to go it alone and to resort to deviousness. It seems likely that he had heard about the men who passed out in federal uniforms with the roll callers. For his master stroke he determined to attempt a daring variation on the ploy. The lieutenant not only secured a genuine blue uniform but also fashioned a prop rifle with a wooden stock and a tin barrel. During the evening of January 15, 1865, Pierce told a sentinel that the prisoners in Block 8—his block—were planning an escape that night at eight o'clock. Shortly before the announced hour, a guard force descended on the block and instituted a thorough search for ladders and other tools. Finding none, they decided the report was false. As they departed, Pierce, in his uniform, fell in with them. They were almost to the gate when an officer asked Charlie where his cartridge box was. Didn't he realize that it was a flagrant violation of orders to enter the prison yard without it? Pierce explained that he had forgotten it in the rush to turn out to get to the barracks. At that point another member of the squad observed, "That's a hell of a gun you've got anyhow." With that, the game was up. Pierce found himself in Colonel Hill's office. Despite the recent escapes, Hill reportedly "laughed very heartily when the case was laid before him," declaring his intention to send the fake weapon to P. T. Barnum.[19]

The most famous Johnson's Island escape plot occurred in late 1864. The elaborate affair involved the potential release of the prisoners as well as possible attacks upon various Lake Erie cities. The scheme had its genesis in April, when President Jefferson Davis dispatched Jacob Thompson, who had served as secretary of the interior during the James Buchanan administration, along with two other agents, to Canada. Once there, Thompson received word to "carry out the instructions you have received from me verbally." What those previous instructions were cannot be determined positively. What Thompson did is clear. The Confederate agent hatched a plot to capture the *Michigan,* the steamer that provided security for Johnson's Island.[20]

In July Thompson sent Capt. Charles H. Cole, formerly of Gen. Nathan Bedford Forrest's Cavalry Corps, to Sandusky. Posing as the secretary of a Pennsylvania oil company, Cole became a fixture in Sandusky society. He befriended officers from the *Michigan,* gaining from them such information as he could. Cole apparently enlisted Sandusky residents sympathetic to the South. He also made arrangements for several more conspirators to arrive by train at Sandusky the night the plot was to be carried out. Finally, Cole met with John Yates Beall, whom Thompson had selected to assist Cole with the project. The two men set the night of September 19 to put their plan into effect. On that evening Beall was to capture a vessel on the lake and direct it toward the *Michigan.* Cole would be aboard the Union ironclad, having scheduled a "wine drinking" with the officers. According to Thompson's subsequent report to Judah Benjamin, the Confederate secretary of state, once the *Michigan* was captured, a cannon shot through the officers' quarters at Johnson's Island "was to signify to the prisoners that the hour for their release had come." Somehow, the prisoners would be mounted, making their way to Virginia via Cleveland and Wheeling.[21]

The plot began to fall apart on September 17, when one of the conspirators betrayed the plan. He was Godfrey J. Hyams, a former Confederate soldier who had become a refugee in Canada and a spy for Union officials.

The man sought out Lt. Col. Bennett Hill, commander of the District of Michigan. "These plots are being constantly made here," Hill later reported, but the earnestness of the informant impressed him. He decided to alert Capt. John C. Carter of the *Michigan*. The informant also apparently revealed Cole's involvement in the plot because, after conferring with Colonel Hill at Johnson's Island, Carter had Cole arrested. Cole cooperated, revealing the identities of his Sandusky coconspirators and telling officials about the pending arrival by rail of some fifty others.[22]

Unaware of these developments, Beall and a group of men he had enlisted seized two Lake Erie passenger ferries, the *Philo Parsons* and the *Island Queen*. The unusual activity on the lake aroused the suspicion of John Brown Jr., son of the fanatic abolitionist, who owned a vineyard on South Bass Island. With three other men, Brown rowed across a dangerously choppy lake from Put-in-Bay to warn Colonel Hill at Johnson's Island that something was afoot. Beall's first inkling that something had gone wrong came when he failed to receive an expected signal from Cole. Although he wanted to see the plan through, the majority of his crew did not. By a vote of 17–2, their view prevailed. They attempted—unsuccessfully—to scuttle both vessels before returning safely to Canada. Cole was confined at Fort Lafayette in New York Harbor, where he remained until 1866. Beall was captured near the Niagara River in western New York on December 16, 1864. He was convicted as a spy and hanged on February 24, 1865.[23]

Despite Thompson's contention that a cannon shot from the *Michigan* was intended to alert the Johnson's Island prisoners to their impending liberation, there is no evidence that they were involved in the plot. Indeed, prison diarists recorded events as if it was all news to them. "Yankees terribly frightened at the discovery of a plot to capture the Michigan (Gun Boat) and release the prisoners confined here," Edmund Patterson wrote on September 21. He added, "I hope they will try it again." John Joyes wrote, "Great excitement prevails in regard to a supposed conspiracy to relieve all of the prisoners on this island by sympathizers. It is believed in the 'Bull Pen' to be a hoax." When a group of men was brought to the island from Sandusky on September 20, the prisoners first thought they had been arrested for opposing the draft. Only later, noted William Peel, did they learn that "they were implicated, or supposed to be, in a scheme to take the island and release the prisoners. There seems to have been such a project on foot," he added.[24]

For the prisoners it was a lost opportunity, the only one of this sort they would have. Its failure meant the Johnson's Island captives would be facing some eight months more at the Sandusky depot, including one more Lake Erie winter; and thanks to a policy of retaliation instituted by the Union in late May 1864, cutting rations some twenty percent, those months would seem even longer.

9

"The Wrath of Hunger"

Rations and Union Retaliation

In general there were two methods of preparing and eating rations at Union prison camps. At about half of the depots, including Camp Chase, Camp Douglas, and Camp Morton, the prisoners cooked and ate in their barracks. A similar system was in place at Rock Island, where the Confederate captives ate in rooms that were connected to their barracks. At Fort Delaware and Elmira, separate mess halls went up at the same time barracks were erected. Mess halls were also built at Point Lookout, largely because Stanton refused to allow barracks to be constructed to replace the tents in which prisoners were housed. The latter system was preferred by medical inspectors. They complained of improperly prepared food, a great deal of waste, and the smoke and fumes that necessarily filled the barracks when the prisoners did their own cooking.[1]

For most of the war, prisoners at Johnson's Island prepared their own meals. As at other camps, they took turns performing mess chores for their blocks. It was a duty that Edmund Patterson dreaded. After completing his duties on August 26, 1863, he wrote, "Each day we have three men detailed whose duty it is to set the table[s], clear them off, sweep the room, scour the knives and forks, receive and divide the rations, and etc., and all this to do three times during the day, and this is what I have been doing today, and those who have had experience in the matter will agree that it is no small job, where there are between eighty and one hundred men to feed."[2]

Writing the same week, John Dooley reported that there were cooking stoves at each end of the block. The meals were served on "very unsteady wooden tables." According to J. L. Stockdale, the tables were pine. The prisoners, he added, were all supplied with a tin plate, tin cup, knife, and fork. They also had buckets for water and wash basins, which they purchased themselves. Dooley added that, thanks to an abundance of funds, he and his messmates ate well. "I strained every nerve to enjoy the bountiful supply underneath which our table groaned and even at times fell down" he wrote.[3]

On July 23, 1864, Surgeon Charles T. Alexander, a medical inspector dispatched by Hoffman, recommended the erection of two large mess halls at Johnson's Island. In his opinion, this would improve both the policing and the health of the camp. Officials had ignored similar suggestions at other prisons, but this time Hoffman acted. Five days after receiving Alexander's report, the commissary general ordered Hill to have the structures built. As he did with virtually every project, Hoffman wanted the work to be done quickly and cheaply. The floors, he instructed, were to be either gravel or "rough board." He wanted them equipped with "farmer's boilers." Hoffman was obsessed with these large cooking devices, and he urged all commandants to utilize them. They used much less fuel than did camp kettles and stoves, keeping with Hoffman's penchant for frugality.

The mess halls were completed on September 3. However, Lieutenant Colonel Scovill refused to occupy them because the roofs leaked badly. This problem was resolved, and the superintendent of prisons soon reported that they resulted in "a decided improvement in the police of [the] quarters." He did recommend that wounded prisoners and those missing limbs be permitted to cook and eat in their blocks because of the difficulty they had in getting to the new facilities.[4]

What the mess halls did not do was improve the quality of the rations the prisoners received. "Provision to day is spoiled and can not be eaten," John Porter complained of one issue. "The generous Yankees always feed us well, they say, yet here is truth to be pushed in their teeth. Do our men at Richmond give yankees spoiled provisions?" In fairness to Johnson's Island officials, records cited above demonstrate that Colonel Hill dealt harshly with suppliers who sent unsatisfactory provisions. This was Porter's only complaint of inferior rations in some nine months of diary entries. It is also very unlikely that Porter would have traded his rations at Johnson's Island for those received by Union prisoners at any Confederate camp.[5]

Virgil Murphey was more specific in his observations of inferior rations. "The bread is baked outside at a prison bakery and supplied to us daily," he wrote. "The bread is not light airy and crispy but heavy and of a liquid mushy character. The authorities doubtless think it is much better and more preferable than any we can make," he continued. "In this they are sadly in error." Murphey further complained of "the want of variety so essential to the proper health and preservation of the human system." In particular, he observed, "The want of vegetables produces constipation almost incurable and soon undermines the system and leaves it vulnerable to all diseases."[6]

During the summer of 1864, the quantity of rations became the big issue with the prisoners. Reports of poor conditions in Confederate prisons had begun to reach the North, prompting Union officials to consider a policy of retaliation against Southern captives. The first significant discussion of such a policy came in late 1863. The commander of a Union parole camp near Annapolis, Maryland reported that prisoners arriving from Richmond were "in a pitiable condition" because of "extreme suffering from a want (apparently) of proper food." When the report reached Stanton, he demanded that Gen. Ethan Allen Hitchcock, the Union commissioner of exchange, determine exactly how Union prisoners were being treated. He was then directed to "take measures for precisely the same treatment toward all prisoners held by the United States, in respect to food, clothing, medical treatment, and other necessities." Hitchcock advised against such a policy. His concerns were not humanitarian but practical. The commissioner feared retaliation might lead to uprisings at Camp Chase, Camp Morton, and other prisons "where the means of security are very slender."[7]

Stanton trod carefully. On December 1 he ordered the sutler stands closed at six major prisons. Johnson's Island, however, was not included. At the end of the month, the war secretary reopened them after hearing that the treatment of Union captives in Richmond had "been materially improved." The order nevertheless placed limits on what the prisoners could purchase. Shoes and underclothing were the only items of clothing permitted. Several food items were allowed, including vegetables, canned meats, and fish.[8]

The respite proved temporary. More reports of alleged Southern abuse were reaching Stanton's office. On May 1, 1864, he sent Hoffman to Annapolis to report on the condition of four hundred sick parolees. The commissary general found the officers generally to be in good condition. The plight of the enlisted men, however, was such that it moved the normally staid officer. He reported, "Some of these poor fellows were wasted to mere skeletons and had scarcely life enough remaining to appreciate that they were now in the hands of friends." Hoffman concluded, "That our soldiers when in the hands of the rebels are starved to death cannot be denied." His advice was blunt. "I would very respectfully urge that retaliatory measures be at once instituted by subjecting the officers we now hold as prisoners of war to a similar treatment."[9]

Perhaps Hoffman was speaking from the heart. Perhaps he was simply offering a suggestion he knew his boss would appreciate. In either event, Stanton quickly acted upon the commissary general's report and its call for retaliation. In a May 5 report to President Lincoln, he asserted that "our prisoners are undergoing ferocious barbarity or the more horrible death of starvation." He urged that Southern officers receive "precisely the same rations and treatment" to which he believed Confederates were subjecting Union captives. The next day, in a message sent to all Union prison commanders, Hoffman hinted at things to come. "It is possible that from circumstances which may soon occur more than ordinary vigilance will be required from the troops in charge of prisoners of war." He urged that guard duty be performed "in the strictest manner."[10]

On May 19 Hoffman submitted a proposal to Stanton calling for a twenty percent reduction in the rations issued to Confederate prisoners. Although Stanton had only called for retaliation against officers, he did not object to Hoffman's recommendation that it apply to all Southern captives. At the suggestion of General Halleck, who was then serving as Lincoln's military chief of staff, tea, coffee, and sugar were eliminated from prisoner rations. On May 27 Stanton formally approved the plan. Retaliation had become the official policy of the Union. On August 10 sutlers were prohibited from selling food or clothing items to the prisoners. Also, friends and relatives could no longer send food to prisoners except in cases of illness. They could only send limited items of clothing to "destitute prisoners" with the approval of the camp commandant.[11]

Among the first prison diary keepers at any camp to take notice of the changes was William Peel. "I understand our rations, already quite limited enough for those who have not the means of purchasing from the Sutler, are to be very materially shortened," Peel wrote on June 5. Three days later he reported that this prison rumor was true. In early August, apparently short on funds, Peel lamented, "I have been, for a week past, confined strictly to Govt rations, & my experience is that a man thus dependent, must be a very small eater not to suffer from hunger." A meat ration, he explained, had been issued Saturday. Intended to last the men three days, it got them only through Sunday's breakfast. After that the prisoners in Peel's block were limited to a small amount of bread.[12]

Edmund Patterson at first attempted to put the changes in a positive light. Noting the absence of coffee and sugar, he observed, "I know we will be healthier without them, especially the villainous compound called coffee." By the time the limits on sutler sales came, Patterson was far less optimistic. "I am afraid that there will be much suffering this winter if the order is enforced, for the rations we receive from the Yankees are not sufficient to keep body and soul together."[13]

Virgil Murphey was more specific. "The ration is entirely insufficient in quantity and quality, and much suffering and distress follows," he wrote soon after arriving in December 1864. "I have frequently enjoyed a piece of bread with as much zest and natural relish as a French connoisseur ever did the most delicious dish." Murphey continued, "I have seen men at the mess hall when the bread was divided and issued catch and gather with ravenous delight the crumbs that fell from the knife. Every atom and particle is carefully and miserly husbanded to appease the wrath of hunger, and enough to subsist a rat is never wasted or destroyed."[14]

"The Yankees are cutting us short on the bread question," Robert Bingham wrote the same month. "We get just about half enough. Enough to keep body & soul together, I suppose, but we eat all we get in two meals & I never have enough." Realizing that he was writing for posterity, Bingham concluded, "This is a real fact, not put here to make you cry when you read it, but to remind me and you in after days of the fact that I actually suffered hunger in a Yankee prison."[15]

Prisoners' accounts of exactly what their rations included varied somewhat. On November 18 J. L. Stockdale described them as "four small hard crackers and two ounces of beef, or one ounce of salt pork, the beef very poor, to each man a day, with three pints of corn hominy, one pint of sugar and one pint of bean to six men for the week." A few weeks earlier, William Peel wrote, "The Yankees give us Ten ozs. of salt pork, or Fifteen of white fish, or [one] lb of fresh or salt beef & [one] lb of bread per day, & an addition of half a pt. of rice, hominy or beans pr week." Apparently this was the ideal ration, because he added, "Instead of receiving the above rations, they are often much less. Our bread sometimes does not exceed 12 ozs. & the meat is often ¼ or ½ short."[16]

The white fish that Peel mentioned appears to have been limited to the prisoners at Camp Chase and Johnson's Island. It was not popular at either location. On September 8 Patterson recorded, "No rations today but bread and rotten fish, which we would none of us eat only as a matter of necessity to keep soul and body together; not a particle of meat or grease of any kind to cook them with, and so salt[y] that we have to boil them in three waters, and when they are finally cooked there is about as much nutriment in them as there would be in the same quantity of boiled shavings." Lt. T. B. Jackson later wrote, "This salted fish was about as palatable and juicy as smoked codfish."[17]

For prisoners of independent means, including a large number of the officers confined at Johnson's Island, the limits placed on boxes received from family members and sutler purchases worked a greater hardship than the reduced rations. One prisoner wrote, "The excitement about the cutting off of our rations & Express has created a great deal of talk & indignation. . . . And great was the indignation & Many the curses heaped upon the Yankees." At least one Yankee, however, was spared the curses of the prisoners. Two days after the order was issued, several boxes arrived for the prisoners. According to Peel, despite orders to the contrary, an un-named lieutenant "gave, apparently intentional, opportunities to us for carrying off unobserved, a good many things & as this diary is designed as a plain record of facts, I don't see that I am at liberty to close my remarks on the occurrences of this day until I shall have acknowledged that my prospect for biscuit & ham for breakfast is highly flattering." It would prove to be the last such prospect for several weeks.[18]

Even with their options severely limited, the resourceful Confederate prisoners occasionally found ways of supplementing their rations. One group decided to tap one of the many maple trees in the prison yard. After two days they had collected about seven gallons of sap. Their intention was to produce maple syrup, but the Southerners were admittedly "inexperienced" in this area. Instead they ended up with "about two pounds of a very tolerable quality of maple sugar." As summer approached, several blocks planted gardens. On September 4 John Washington Inzer wrote that he had enjoyed some turnips from a fellow prisoner's garden. Despite the government's policy of retaliation, camp officials did not interfere. Lake Erie's climate, however, produced another concern. On September 17 Peel observed "some of the finest tomato bushes here I ever saw." They were not yet ripe, and he feared "the frost will catch them."[19]

It did not take long for the hungry prisoners to resort to less palatable options. Perhaps the most common was eating rats. The rodents were common at every prison compound, and diary entries describing the activity are too common to leave any doubt that hundreds were consumed. On September 14 John Dooley observed, "Rats are found to be very good for food, and every night many are captured and slain. So pressing is the want of food that nearly all who can have gone into the rat business, either selling these horrid animals or killing and eating them." The rodents were so tame, Dooley added, that capturing them was easy. Three days later, Patterson wrote that hunger had driven him to accept a friend's invitation to dine on a rat stew. "I cannot say that I am particularly fond of them," he noted, "but rather than go hungry I will eat them when I can get them." He added, "They taste very much like young squirrel and would be good enough if called by any other name." After trying his first rat on November 25, Peel admitted, "They proved quite palatable in my half starved condition."[20]

No animal that wondered into the camp was safe. At the same time, not every prisoner could bring himself to partake. E. John Ellis found this out when he visited Block 12 and discovered a freshly cooked cat. "I placed it close enough to my olfactories to get the scent and was tempted to taste it," he wrote, "but my prejudices were too strong."[21]

Hunger drove a number of Johnson's Island prisoners—and their comrades at other Union depots—to make another unpalatable choice. As rations decreased, the number of prisoners choosing to take the oath of allegiance to the Union increased. The collapse of the exchange cartel also factored into the decision. Although prisoners taking the oath were not released, they did receive the promise of extra rations and better quarters.

They also earned the enduring enmity of their fellow prisoners. This concerned both Colonel Hill and Lieutenant Colonel Scovill. On September 5, 1864, Hill informed Hoffman, "There has been a persistent effort to intimidate men in the prison who show the least disposition to yield to the United States Government. Their roommates drive them out of quarters [during the] nights, and personal violence is not only threatened but often inflicted upon those who are suspected of wishing to take the oath of amnesty." In his inspection report for the following week, the superintendent of prisons recommended that oath takers be separated. His suggestion was to erect a small building to house them. In forwarding the report to Hoffman, Colonel Hill proposed instead that one of the barracks already in place be set aside for their use. "If they had one of the barracks by themselves I presume it would be filled," Hill wrote. "At present but a very few dare let their sentiments be known." Hoffman responded that there would be no objection to removing the oath takers to a separate barracks. He suggested housing them in a block close to the guardhouse.[22]

The concerns expressed by Scovill and Hill were valid. Nine months earlier, several prisoners had learned the identity of a "traitor" and pursued him as a Union lieutenant attempted to escort him out of the compound. According to one witness, the man was "hooted, snow-balled and used roughly—and as he neared the gate he increased his pace indicating his desire to get out of the way of the infuriated officers, who no doubt would have hung him." One prisoner explained, "Both he & the Yankee officer got a pretty good pelting with snowballs—all the rocks were frozen to the ground." The lieutenant called out a guard force for assistance.[23]

The indignation peaked in January 1865, when Block 1 was set aside as quarters for the oath takers. This particular barracks was considered to be prime prison real estate. It was divided into small rooms, each with its own stove. In addition, according to William Peel, "the [original] occupants of the small rooms have gone to a good deal of expense, such as papering, fixing up bunks &c. &c., all of which the authorities here have sanctioned, & now they are to be turned out & their places to be filled by these oath takers & skulkers out of the service." Copying the order into his diary, Virgil Murphey added, "Read if you can control your indignation and conceal your disgust for these miserable craven hearted wretches."[24]

On January 30 the move began. "Crowds gathered upon the boulevard of the prison to scrutinize their faces, learn who they were and what states they represented," Murphey wrote. "They marched amid horrid groans and biting sarcasm with penitent heads abjectly bowed, eyes fastened intently upon the earth as if it would open its ponderous jaws and swallow them for apostasy, with pal[l]id looks indicating their fear of vengenace." Peel wrote, "The yard rings with derisions that are heaped upon them as they pass along." One man, unable to face the reception, left his block during the night. Unfortunately, he went into the wrong block. The prisoners there, seeing him with all his belongings, figured out his plans, and one "very deliberately kicked him out of the room."[25]

When no men left their blocks, Peel noted, the prisoners began to feel guilty for suspecting two or three of being potential oath takers. The next day, however, "as if by a preconcerted signal," nine suddenly packed their belongings and departed. By February 2, he estimated, fifty-five "traitors" were occupying Block 1. Murphey observed, "Even the Yankees are undisguised in their aversions to these neophytes, for they hate the traitor when benefitted by their treason."[26]

Murphey's views were understandable, and they likely represented those of an overwhelming majority of his fellow captives. Still, among a prison population that ranged from 2,100 to 2,600, it is not surprising that a small percentage became desperate to ameliorate their condition. Although conditions at Johnson's Island were generally better than those at many other Union prisons, life was not easy. Some factors, such as bitter winter weather, were beyond the control of the Union keepers. Others, such as occasionally lax medical care, were not. But all contributed to the decision-making process of the "traitors."

10

"A Pitiful Scene"

Climate and Health

On December 14, 1863, what one prisoner described as a "heavy gale" blew down a barracks that was being constructed for Johnson's Island's Union garrison. It killed at least one man and wounded at least three others. The loss did not trouble the Confederate captives, particularly the diarist who wrote, "Small favors thankfully received, large ones in proportion." The next serious windstorm to strike the island, "hard enough to make these old buildings totter," hit on August 26, 1864. It blew down a maple tree located just outside the fence, taking a fifty-foot section of the fence with it. Two sentinels were knocked from their perches, but neither was seriously hurt. Other guards quickly manned the gap, preventing anyone from escaping. Camp officials had it repaired the next day.[1]

Bad as they were, these storms paled in intensity compared to the one which hit the island between eight and nine o'clock on the evening of September 23, 1864. Likely a tornado of F-1 intensity on the Fujita Scale, it struck from the southwest. According to one prisoner's account, the storm produced a "screaming" sound. Another described "the most awful roaring that I have ever listened to." Several prisoners had retired to their bunks, but few had fallen asleep when the storm hit. They fled the vulnerable blocks, wearing whatever they had on at the moment, and ran out into the yard as quickly as they could. Men in the upper-story rooms jumped through the windows. "I think I touched the floor once between my bunk and the door," Patterson wrote, "and the next jump I landed outside amid the flying timber of Block 4." The wind caught him, and, "I was blown about twenty feet and happened to land on that part of the body 'where mothers smite their young' and took a rather unpleasant ride for some distance until I landed on 'all fours' in a gutter where I was pelted with hail stones, shingles, mud and sand until I was utterly demoralized."[2]

Through the lightning, Patterson watched the storm take the roof from Block 4 "as it would a sheet of tissue paper." Timber from the buildings became missiles. "Trees [were] tossed wildly to & fro," Peel wrote, "the tops of many of them being wrung off & swept furiously through the air to the distance of many rods." Prisoners, Patterson added, were "rolling and tumbling over each other, picked up and tossed about by the wind at its pleasure."[3]

The tornado unroofed Blocks 4, 5, and 9 as well as one wing of the prison hospital. Four large trees were blown down, and one of the new mess halls was "badly canted over." Large sections of fence were "made a perfect wreck," according to Hill's report. Peel wrote that the "fence along the entire West side of the yard [was] leveled to the ground." A guard force hastily deployed to man the breach, and several nervous sentries fired randomly into the yard. Both Patterson and Peel wrote that, despite some close calls, none of the shots struck a prisoner. However, writing twenty-seven years later, Isaiah G. W. Steedman, a Confederate surgeon and prisoner, offered a different view. "We surgeons were kept busy the balance of the night, dressing the wounds of our comrades, who were either wounded by flying timbers or the bullets of our frightened or demoralized guards."[4]

Peel was up early the next morning, visiting Block 5 to see how friends he had there had fared. They were well, but he learned that two men in the block had been seriously hurt. Patterson, who was housed in Block 5, wrote that one of them suffered a broken thigh and had a large section of flesh torn off when he was struck by a rafter that flew from Block 4. Many had sore feet from stepping on nails as they returned to the block. "It is nothing less than a miracle that no one was killed," Peel wrote, concluding, "I think I would prefer fighting a battle every morning before breakfast rather than experience a repetition of last night's work."[5]

To prison officials at Johnson's Island, it must have appeared equally miraculous that not a single prisoner escaped as a result of the storm. According to Peel, a North Carolina captain tried two nights later. The fence was still down, and the officer crawled to within a few yards of the guard line. He lay in a turnip patch, awaiting his opportunity to slip by. The plan went awry when a Union corporal stepped into the garden. He was trying for a turnip, Peel noted, but instead "took away a full-grown Rebel." In an article written thirty years after the fact, Capt. W. Gart Johnson claimed that a Virginian tied three planks together shortly after the storm struck and made his way to the lake. He floated for several hours but was never able to navigate to the mainland.[6]

Rainy weather for the next week slowed repair work, although Peel observed that it did not keep the Yankees from expediting repairs to their portion of the compound. Of course wet weather made roof repairs all the more urgent to the prisoners. Discouraged by the slow pace, they quickly took matters into their own hands. In addition to checking on friends, the resourceful Confederates gathered up as much lumber and as many nails as they could scavenge the morning after the storm. "The Yanks stopped us as soon as possible," Peel wrote, "but not until numerous planks had been stowed away." Over the next few days, stealing supplies became a game with the captives. They could not repair their own roofs under the watchful eyes of the guards, but they could fix up bunks and add partitions to their blocks. Generally they secured lumber by sending out a shill to pick up a large plank. A sentinel would step in to stop him, and as the pair argued, other prisoners would sneak behind him to gather as many pieces as they could. One particularly clever captive managed to tie pieces of clothesline to several planks and draw them in after dark. Despite the delays, Scovill reported on October 2 that all the blocks were again under roof, except for Block 5. He expected all the work to be completed the following day.[7]

Although far less dramatic, Lake Erie's cold winters posed a more serious threat to the Southern prisoners than did tornadoes. Unlike other Union prisons, there is no evidence of any Johnson's Island captive freezing to death. There is, however, strong evidence of suffering. On January 25, 1865, Virgil Murphey reported that the temperature had reached two degrees below zero. As a result, he noted, the prisoners were frozen "almost into a lethargic state." In a letter that may have been smuggled out of camp, prisoner Daniel S. Printup explained to his wife, "I myself have experienced colder weather but at least half of the prisoners never before knew what it was to be exposed to cold more than a few degrees below the freezing point. These suffered & could hardly realize the fact that cold could be so intense." As winter weather stretched well into the spring, John Porter simply became angry, writing in his diary, "Snowing all yesterday—2nd of May—What a country. Yanks."[8]

The suffering was perhaps the greatest on the night of January 1, 1864. It was a cold snap that survived in people's memories well into the twentieth century, according to climate historians Thomas and Jeanne Schmidlin, whose book *Thunder in the Heartland* recounts significant weather events in Ohio's history. The bitter cold was not limited to Ohio. At Camp Douglas near Chicago, prison diarists wrote that both prisoners and guards suffered terribly. One Rock Island prisoner placed the temperature at twenty-eight below, while another had it three degrees colder. The latter wrote that water froze within five feet of the stove in his barracks. At both Illinois camps, snow accompanied the frigid temperatures.[9]

At Johnson's Island, snow, sleet, and rain ushered in the new year. By morning the precipitation had stopped but not the cold. At daylight J. L. Stockdale placed the temperature at four degrees. By dark, Stockdale wrote, it had plummeted to minus twenty-four. "The sentries, half frozen," James Mayo observed, "are releaved every hour and proceed to the block houses to thaw themselves out." Even in a small room with a fire burning, water froze. According to Robert Bingham, the ice on the windows of his block was half an inch think. Stockdale, Bingham, and Mayo were all among parties of prisoners that camp officials allowed to go outside the compound for extra wood. Although their sojourn was brief, all reported that comrades returned with severely frostbitten fingers. Stockdale feared that a member of his party would lose an ear to frostbite. It was from one of these parties that Captain Boyd decided to return to the island after attempting to escape. John M. Porter may have been the only prisoner to view the situation philosophically, writing, "All of nature's powers seem to be taken up in order to bring to our minds by this temperature that man's works are finite."[10]

The cold soon exacted a price. "Cold weather continues, ice two feet thick on the lake," Stockdale noted on January 11. "Many prisoners are sick with pneumonia and influenza, some cases of typhoid, three or four die a day." Three days later Mayo wrote, "A great many are sick in the Hospital and some die nearly every day." According to official returns, twenty prisoners died at Johnson's Island during January 1864. Another seventeen died the next month. In March the death toll was ten. As the weather moderated, so too did the number of deaths. For the remaining nine months of 1864, a total of twenty-four prison deaths was recorded.[11]

Exacerbating the often bitter weather at Johnson's Island were the frequent shortages of wood. Soon after arriving in the fall of 1864, Virgil Murphey wrote, "Wood we receive daily and furnished with an axe and saw we have to cut and split it to suit ourselves." He added that the prisoners received a sufficient amount, but that was a minority view. Robert

Bingham wrote of observing prisoners "working at old stumps around the yard to get a little wood." In early November 1864 John Joyes complained that the prisoners had received no wood for several days. The previous autumn, Stockdale had noted the arrival of stoves for the blocks but added, "We can have fire if they will let us have wood." During the cold months that followed, he frequently complained about the lack of wood.[12]

Securing water also proved difficult for Johnson's Island prisoners. In late 1863 John Dooley and J. L. Stockdale both wrote of long lines at the pumps of the two wells that supplied the entire prison. Often one of the pumps was out of order, lengthening the wait considerably. As Dooley noted, "[the] water being clearer in the morning we try to furnish each room with a supply of drinking water for the day; but after some few thousands of buckets have been plunged in these holes the water becomes troubled and muddy and may only be used for washing and cooking purposes."[13]

By December the pumps were freezing. Robert Bingham complained in his diary that he had been trying for several days to wash his clothes but had been thwarted by a lack of water. The situation became so desperate that prison officials let a few men at a time, under a heavy guard, go to the lake for water. They had to break through six inches of ice, but it was well worth the effort to avoid the wells and what former prisoner B. L. Farinholt termed their "intolerable liquid." Farinholt later recalled, "O what a boon it was considered by those who for weeks and months had not known the taste of pure water! What an eager throng waited at the opening of the large southern gate, which opened from the stockade to the lake shore!"[14]

In January 1864, Gen. Isaac R. Trimble, one of the most prominent prisoners on the island, wrote a letter to Terry. In it he made a number of complaints, ranging from trigger-happy sentinels to the inability of the prisoners to make purchases. The well water, Trimble wrote, was "unwholesome and of nauseous taste." An inspecting officer assigned by Terry to investigate the grievances wrote, "The subject of water demands attention." He agreed that the well water was "not suitable as a beverage, as it causes a diarrhea which invariably proves fatal."[15]

Despite this dire warning, it was six months before any action was contemplated to address the problem. In June Hill took some "crude measurements" for a proposed waterworks. He then hired a civil engineer, who reported that a system that would supply about thirty-two gallons a day to five thousand men would cost $7,080. A medical inspector sent by Hoffman in June endorsed the proposal, but he conceded that the commissary general would disapprove it "as it involves a large expenditure." Apparently he was right. Although Hoffman ordered Hill to "have your water pipes put in good condition," there is no record of him approving the project. In September an inspector from the Army's Northern Department reported that the problem still existed. This was despite the fact that the plans had been submitted and "this recommendation has been repeatedly made." As late as December 1864, one prison diarist was reporting that his comrades were making two daily trips to the lake to obtain water. He added, however, that the water was "both healthy and well tasted."[16]

Despite these problems, Johnson's Island was the healthiest of Union prisons. Its mortality rate was far lower than that of any other Northern depot. Despite that, when Dr. Clark, Hoffman's fastidious medical inspector, returned in early January 1864, he found areas for complaint. Sinks, kitchens, and prison quarters he termed "filthy." In addition, Clark noted, "the grounds show no evidence of having been policed for a long time." The doctor was, however, satisfied with the rations, blankets, and clothing provided to the prisoners. Clark offered a mixed opinion of hospital facilities. He found the supplies of blankets, medicines, and other items to be good. He also commended the quality of the hospital rations. Clark was less pleased with the policing of the hospital. He also called for better ventilation, an additional heating stove, and laundry facilities. Dr. Woodbridge was still the surgeon in charge, and the inspector praised his "professional ability" and "gentle temper." Unfortunately, the latter trait, in Clark's opinion, "renders him unfit to force obedience to his orders in the proper conduct of the hospital or in the sanitary management of the camp."[17]

The poor policing of the depot was also emphasized by Dr. Alexander, who visited the facility in July 1864. He blamed the situation for a recent sharp increase in cases of dysentery. It was this report that led to the construction of the new kitchens, which Clark proposed as a way of improving policing in the blocks. "The hospital was in good condition," he informed Hoffman, "well policed; the sick in every way sufficiently well provided for."[18]

The question of proper policing came up frequently at Union prisons. Dr. Clark termed the prisoners at Fort Delaware "indolent," and Alexander wrote of the same facility, "The quarters of the prisoners are fairly policed and could be kept in good condition if the inmates were not too lazy to consult even self-interest and comfort." The same concerns existed at Johnson's Island. Writing of the poor policing among the prisoners, Scovill noted, "The difficulty of getting this work done without a resort to brute force to compel it is the greatest the superintendent has to contend with." Alexander concurred with his assessment, expressing both surprise and disgust that "men calling themselves gentlemen should be willing to live in such filth."[19]

The prisoners' opinions regarding the quality of hospital facilities at Johnson's Island were as mixed as those of the inspectors. After visiting friends and observing Confederate surgeon prisoners, Peel wrote that they did "all that skill in their profession, a boundless energy, & an untiring zeal in the prosecution of their good work could accomplish." Other prisoners, serving as nurses, were "fully alive to their every duty." Virgil Murphey shared Peel's opinion. "The Hospital for accommodation of our sick, under the immediate charge of rebel physicians, is one of the best regulated institutions I ever saw," he wrote. "Those men who have devoted their time and attention so exclusively to the welfare and comfort of our invalids deserve great credit and honor."[20]

Robert Bingham held a different view, terming the hospital "a disgrace to the Yankee nation & an outrage to humanity." He wrote that the sick received "butcher rations—musty rice, beans, tough beef & pork twice a week & coffee that gives any body that uses it the diarrhoea." He later moderated his views somewhat, noting that the beds had new sheets and pillows. He added that "the officers who attend to it are worth all the surgeons in the army." Although not critical of the facility itself, Thomas Taylor wrote, "The hospital presents a pitiful scene, so many anxious yet hopeless looking faces all showing such yearning for domestic sympathy and attention." Following his escape, R. D. Chapman wrote of the facility, "The hospital was furnished with no delicacies for the sick, except what could be procured by the prisoners; the medicines were quite inadequate to the command."[21]

Perhaps the most balanced view of the Johnson's Island hospital was that of Dr. Isaiah G. W. Steedman. One of the Confederate surgeons Peel included in his praise, Colonel Steedman, of the 1st Alabama Artillery, had been captured at Port Hudson, Louisiana, in 1863. After a brief stay at the Governor's Island prison, he arrived at Johnson's Island in October 1863. He was soon put in charge of the prison hospital.

Writing in 1891, Steedman remembered that both Dr. Woodbridge and his successor, Dr. Henry Eversman, "did their duty as humane men; while they could not change or disobey orders from higher authority, they did their best to ameliorate our condition." As for the challenges faced by the doctors, Steedman wrote, "Chronic bowel diseases, the greatest enemy of armies, and especially prisons, prevailed to an alarming extent . . . Prison diet and treatment could do nothing for it; inevitable slow death awaited its victims."[22]

The extent to which Union officials were culpable for sickness and death in Northern prisons is open to debate. In one area, however, it is beyond doubt that they did too little. At various times, medical inspectors reported cases of scurvy at Point Lookout, Elmira, Camp Morton, Fort Delaware, and Johnson's Island. At Johnson's Island the number of cases was small, accounting for less than two percent of reported diseases. Still, there was no reason for any cases to occur. Hoffman frequently criticized camp commanders for minor mistakes in reports they sent him. However, there is almost no record of the commissary general of prisoners issuing orders to arrest this highly preventable disease.

In January 1864 Clark reported from Johnson's Island that "although there are no declared cases of this disease at present in camp, . . . many, perhaps a majority of the prisoners, are more or less tainted with it." Writing Terry a week later, Hoffman made no mention of scurvy. His only reference to Clark's inspection was an insistence that the prisoners be required to police the camp. Seven months later Alexander reported that the disease had actually broken out at the prison. Hoffman again ignored the situation. Writing to Hill this time, he repeated his call for better policing, complained about the sutler system, ordered that the sinks be improved, and called for the erection of a washhouse. According to Steedman, Dr. Alexander did all he could to address the issue. "Whenever he visited our prison, and the wholesale prevalence of scurvy was exhibited to him, he promptly and cheerfully ordered additional rations of fresh meat and vegetables, especially onions and cabbages."[23]

Even these actions may not have been enough. When the policy of retaliation was eased in early 1865, and the sutler once again could sell vegetables to the prisoners, John Reece welcomed the news. "A good [many prisoners] have the scurvy and some are very bad off, teeth all becoming loose and sores breaking out on the legs," he wrote. "One pretty bad case in my room."[24]

The most dreaded disease among the prisoners was smallpox. Although there were outbreaks at almost every Union prison, the degree varied a great deal. Camp Chase, Elmira, Rock Island, and Alton were among the Northern camps that experienced severe outbreaks. Johnson's Island was largely spared, but not altogether. On October 17, 1863, Pierson informed Hoffman that prisoners transferred from other depots had arrived with the disease. There were seven cases in the "pest house," he reported. On November 1, J. L. Stockdale wrote in his diary that there were "several new cases" of the disease. He repeated the entry as late as January 17, 1864.[25]

In November 1864 camp officials received reports of an outbreak of smallpox in Sandusky. Hill ordered that intercourse between the camp and the city be limited. The adjutant general in Sandusky received orders to severely limit passes to the island. The last reference to the disease came in January 22, 1865. Less than a month before his own death from pneumonia, William Peel briefly noted in his diary that there were "several cases now on hand."[26]

By that time, although they may not have realized it, prisoners who had survived their stay at Johnson's Island thus far had a good chance of seeing home again. It was the last winter of the Confederacy. The cause for which they had fought was close to becoming the Lost Cause. The best hope now for Southern prisoners was a trip back to Dixie.

11

"Sad and Glad at the Same Time"

The Road to Release

As 1864 neared its end, it was becoming increasingly apparent that the Confederacy's days were numbered. General Grant, now the Union general in chief, had Robert E. Lee's Army of Northern Virginia pinned down in front of Petersburg. William Tecumseh Sherman had taken Atlanta and was cutting a path of destruction across eastern Georgia. The Mississippi River had been under the control of the Union for over a year, and the Northern blockade of the South's ports was effectively sealing off the Confederacy. These factors—combined with the political realities of a presidential election year—helped lead Union officials toward a reconsideration of the exchange question.

To be sure, Grant had become a determined foe of exchange. In 1862, faced with fifteen thousand Fort Donelson prisoners, he had favored immediate parole. For similarly practical reasons, Grant had paroled the Vicksburg garrison the following year. Now, hoping to deliver a knockout blow to a weary Confederacy, the general in chief felt that pragmatism did not favor exchange. Gen. Benjamin Butler had been named "special agent of exchange" by the Union in late 1863. Despite the special enmity the South felt toward him, the publicity-hungry officer had worked tirelessly and apparently sincerely to reach an agreement. Grant counseled caution. As he explained the situation to Butler, "It is hard on our men held in Southern prisons not to exchange them, but it is humanity to those left in the ranks to fight out battles. Every man we hold, when released on parole or otherwise, becomes an active soldier against us at once either directly or indirectly. If we commence a system of exchange which liberates all prisoners taken, we

96

will have to fight on until the whole South is exterminated. If we hold those caught they amount to no more than dead men."[1]

On September 9 Butler made a proposition to Robert Ould, the Confederate commissioner of exchange, that balanced Grant's military concerns with humanitarian considerations. He suggested that the two sides exchange "from time to time" sick and wounded prisoners who would likely remain unfit for duty for sixty days. "I trust and believe," Butler wrote, "that this measure of obvious humanity will meet your agreement." It ended up meeting Ould's agreement, and perhaps more surprising, that of Grant and Stanton as well. On October 2 Hoffman prepared to forward to Point Lookout all prisoners who met the terms of the agreement.[2]

Although Hill did not receive Hoffman's order until October, word apparently reached the camp earlier. On September 15 William Peel wrote, "There was considerable of pleasure & excitement caused this morning by the appearance at the Hospital of Yankee Doctors who announced that their mission was to examine the patients for the purpose of selecting twenty of the worst cases, who were to be sent on exchange to Dixie." The scene was repeated the next day. Four days after that, Peel explained, "The surgeons say they have not received, but are expecting orders to send off those whose health would be likely to be seriously impaired by remaining here through the winter." On October 5 Peel reported that forty-five "sick officers left for Dixie."[3]

As sick and invalid prisoners departed the Northern camps, a number of captives whose condition was as bad—or even worse—arrived to take their place. They came from the Army of Tennessee, commanded by Gen. John Bell Hood, which had suffered severe defeats at the battles of Franklin and Nashville. According to one Union official, the prisoners arrived at Louisville "in a very destitute condition." Their plight moved even Hoffman, who was there at the time. He attempted to secure shoes for them, but Stanton brusquely refused the request.[4]

The prisoners were forwarded to Camp Chase, Camp Douglas, and Johnson's Island. At Camp Douglas the inspecting officer reported that they were "poorly clad, many of them are nearly barefoot, and destitute of blankets." A guard at Camp Chase wrote, "They are the most destitute and spiritless of any perhaps that have arrived here, many of them being entirely barefooted and others suffering from scarcity of clothing." Camp Chase's inspector was even more blunt. On March 11, 1865, he explained, "A very large decrease in numbers of sick and deaths since my last [report] is attributable to the fact that those brought here in an almost dying condition have died."[5]

On December 22 Johnson's Island prisoner John Reece wrote that about five hundred officers had arrived from the Army of Tennessee. The latest "fresh fish" claimed that "the disasters to Hoods army is the worst thing of the war." Many, Reece added, arrived with frostbitten hands. They had fallen on the ice crossing the bay to the camp and landed on their hands, which were not protected by gloves. The same day, John Joyes and other members of his mess invited four of Hood's men into their block. "It almost makes the heart bleed," Joyes wrote, "to witness the scanty apparel with which our poor recruits have to withstand the chilly blasts of a Northern winter."[6]

Destitute Southern prisoners received a small measure of relief in January 1865 as the result of an unusual arrangement made by Union and Confederate officials. On October 30, 1864, Ould sought permission from General Grant to ship a load of cotton north. The cotton would be sold and the proceeds used to purchase clothing for Confederate prisoners. The general in chief immediately endorsed the plan. Administration officials added their consent, likely on the strength of Grant's approval. On November 11 Grant informed Ould that one thousand bales of cotton would be received in New York. As part of the arrangement, the Union would be permitted to send supplies to its prisoners held in the South.[7]

Had matters proceeded in a timely way, the agreement would have prevented a great deal of suffering as another northern winter approached. Unfortunately a number of difficulties plagued the operation. Stanton disapproved of the original Confederate prisoner selected to make arrangements for the sale of the cotton and the subsequent purchase of supplies. He then placed burdensome limits on the activities of the prisoner's replacement. Meanwhile, Union officials in Mobile Bay refused to allow the shipment to clear. Bad weather and a shortage of men to load the cotton slowed things further. As a result, it was January 24, 1865, before the shipment arrived in New York. By then a depressed cotton market limited the amount of money realized from the sale to $331,789.66.[8]

The supplies, which included blankets and clothing, arrived at the Northern prisons in March. At most camps, prison diarists gave the arrival little attention; and those that did generally chose not to elaborate. John Joyes noted on March 17 that the clothing was being distributed at Johnson's Island. The next day John Reece wrote that enough had arrived to supply the needy prisoners. Although he complained that "the articles long and so badly needed never [arrived] here untill yesterday," Reece added that "all were very pleased" with what they received.[9]

By then news that was even more pleasing had reached the prisoners. After countless rumors had raised the hopes of the captives, the two sides finally agreed to resume the exchange of prisoners. By this time Grant had dispatched Butler and was largely handling negotiations himself. On January 13 he approved a proposal made by the Confederates four months earlier that both sides release all prisoners held in close confinement. On February 2 he informed Stanton, "I am endeavoring to make arrangements to exchange about 3,000 prisoners per week." This sudden change in policy did not mean that Grant had abandoned his military concerns. He asked that Confederates from states firmly under Union control be released first. After observing that the Rebels were sending their returned prisoners directly to Lee's army, he instructed Hoffman to make certain that men unfit for duty were sent away before well men.[10]

The news was not long in reaching Johnson's Island prisoners, although the first report was not strictly accurate. "Exchange news a little favorable," John Joyes wrote on February 6. "A statement that three thousand per month have been negotiated for." On the 13th Joyes observed, "Exchange question 'high up,' everybody excited, & every imaginable 'grape.'" The excitement grew higher on the following day, as the compound "thronged with eager listeners to every floating 'grape.'" Two days later he reported that the process had begun, and about one hundred prisoners had left that day. On February 18, according to Joyes, Colonel Hill informed the prisoners that between one and three hundred men would be leaving the prison every week. He recorded the departure of one hundred on the 20th, three hundred on the 24th, and another three hundred on March 1. Because of illness, Joyes may have missed others.[11]

Although skeptical at first, John Dooley also detailed the rumors of the impending exchange. Like Joyes, he reported the first departure on February 16, adding, "The excitement is growing intense." Those departing on the 20th, he wrote, were those who had been captured during May and June 1863, men who had spent nearly two years on the island. Among them was a friend of Dooley's, who promised to tell Dooley's family "to be of good cheer, that I am coming too."[12]

The prediction proved accurate. On February 27 Dooley wrote, "Two hundred prisoners leave and one hundred more to go today and I am among the number—GLORY ALLELUIA!" As the captain rushed to pack his belongings and bid farewell to friends, a messmate blackened the shoes he was to wear on the return journey. In a statement that speaks to the aristocratic attitude held by a number of the Johnson's Island officers, Dooley explained, "Pete has no pride about such things and provided it is for a friend and honorable he cares not what he does."

The parolees walked across the frozen lake to the Sandusky depot. This was a new experience for a large number of the Southerners. Many fell, and according to Dooley, "the poor bewildered fellows are almost tempted to return to prison, so great is the danger of breaking their necks." From Sandusky the liberated captives traveled by rail through Pittsburgh and Harrisburg, reaching Baltimore the next day. From there a steamer took them to Fortress Monroe, Virginia, and up the James River to a flag-of-truce boat. That boat delivered Dooley home to Richmond. Although glad to be home, Dooley noted with concern, "I find nearly all my friends gloomy and despondent in regard to the future of the Confederacy."[13]

The gloom and despondency felt by Dooley's acquaintances in Richmond was soon to grow worse. On April 2, 1865, following a siege of ten months, Robert E. Lee's lines at Petersburg collapsed. The next day Union forces entered the Southern capital. Six days after that, Lee surrendered his Army of Northern Virginia to Grant at Appomattox Court House.

For Confederate prisoners the news meant they would likely be returning home soon, but they would not be returning to an independent Confederacy. "When the news came of Lee's surrender," Capt. W. Gart Johnson later recalled, "we were sad and glad at the same time: sad to know that it had to be, and glad to know that we would soon see our loved ones at home." Diarists there at the time recorded less ambivalence. "What a great fallen set this prison now contains," John Reece observed after the news arrived. Describing the scene, John Joyes wrote, "The Federals are firing a salute of two hundred guns & flags are flying from every house top. The band is playing national airs, and the Rebs are gloomy."[14]

The *Sandusky Register* reported that the oath takers in Block 1 received the news "with loud and repeated cheering." The other prisoners refused to believe the report, believing such an announcement would surely be accompanied by a one-hundred-gun salute. Confirmation, in the form of the two-hundred-gun salute Joyes mentioned and a "jollification," came on April 10. Union barracks were decorated with flags, the post band performed, and the island received a number of visitors. When the American flag was raised over Block 1, a shouting match ensued between the fifty to sixty oath takers and the still loyal Confederates. If the disagreement resulted in any violence, the *Register* did not report it. Indeed, according to the paper, "All engaged in the exercises, will long remember the jollification on the Island."[15]

The mood changed suddenly five days later with the news of the assassination of Abraham Lincoln and the attempted murder of Secretary of State William Henry Seward. John Reece wrote in his diary that Colonel Hill entered the compound and warned the prisoners against expressing approval of the deed "as it might exasperate the guards on the wall and cause them to fire into the prisoners." On April 17 the *Register* reported that Hill had "issued an order to the guard to shoot down the first rebel who exulted over the death of President Lincoln." This brought a vehement denial from the commandant. He termed the report "entirely incorrect" and continued, "In no possible view of the case could I be allowed to forget that the men in my hands were unarmed prisoners, whom it was as much my duty to protect as to retain." Besides, Hill further explained, the prisoners seemed "depressed and sorrowful" at the news. "I know of but two exceptions to this rule."[16]

Prison diarists confirmed Hill's view. "Our officers all regard the death of Mr. L. as a sad blow to our future," Joyes wrote, "for we were fully impressed with the belief that his policy would be lenient." Added Reece, "A great number of the [prisoners] who used to cuss 'old abe' for a perfect tyrant . . . now seem to think he was a very good man after all and so express themselves." John Ellis believed Lincoln was "disposed to be conciliatory and magnanimous." Of the martyred president, he wrote, "He was firm in his purpose and though I was his enemy, I shall ever believe that he was honest and conscientious in all that he did."[17]

Although the conflict was clearly nearing its end, the surrender of Lee's army did not stop the flow of prisoners to Johnson's Island. The Petersburg Campaign produced a number of captives, as did numerous other fights that took place during the war's waning days. Officially, 989 Confederates arrived at the Lake Erie depot during April 1865. Reece recorded the arrival of 450 on April 13 and another 350 seven days later (although the *Register* put the number on the latter date at 331).[18]

Among them was Luther Rice Mills of the 26th Virginia Infantry. Mills was captured on April 6 at the battle of Sayler's Creek. After a brief stay at the Old Capitol Prison, where he learned of the Lincoln assassination,

Mills was among a contingent of prisoners sent on to Johnson's Island. According to his postwar memoirs, he arrived at Sandusky on April 19. Like his predecessors, Mills expressed indignation at the search to which he and his fellow prisoners were subjected. He also complained of poor rations and bedbugs. His stay, however, would prove to be relatively brief.[19]

Samuel Thomas McCullough was another Confederate prisoner who did not reach Johnson's Island until after Lee's surrender. Captured in early April, he too spent a few days at Old Capitol before being sent on to Sandusky. As his train passed through Pittsburgh on its way to Lake Erie, McCullough learned of Lee's surrender. Like Mills, he was irritated by the search process, but he managed to hold on to some items by putting them in his mouth.

McCullough had been at Johnson's Island exactly two weeks when, on April 25, Colonel Hill posted an order on the bulletin board instructing all who wished to take the oath of allegiance to send their applications in immediately. Two days later Hill visited the prison in person "& delivered himself of his views on the subject of taking the oath." Although he did not record the commandant's exact words, McCullough wrote, "His opinions on the subject were very sound, & his views of the reciprocal relations & obligations existing between the Government on the one hand & the citizen on the other, very correct."[20]

For the devoted Confederates, Hill's announcement was a few days premature. As Mills recalled, "The prisoners remained firm in their allegiance until [Gen. Joseph Johnston] surrendered, when it was evident that the Southern Confederacy was a failure, and that they were no longer bound by their oath." Johnston surrendered to Sherman on April 26. The news reached the island three days later, and Joyes observed, "The day is clear and bright but, under our many defeats all prisoners are gloomy indeed. Many applications for the amnesty are being made." On May 1 he added, "Very few among the prisoners refuse to take the amnesty oath. The cause for which we have served faithfully for four years I now regard as hopeless, and further resistance entirely useless." By the 5th he estimated that only 418 of the approximately 2,800 prisoners had not made their application. The next day he noted that "the majority of the surplus reb's have applied since yesterday." On May 8 the *Register* reported that only 35 Johnson's Island prisoners had declined to take the oath.[21]

Regardless of the decisions made by the Confederate prisoners, their fate remained in the hands of Union authorities. On May 8 the War Department announced its policy. All prisoners below the rank of general who had agreed to take the oath of allegiance before the fall of Richmond could be released upon taking the oath. Grant preferred a more sweeping process. Ever practical, the general in chief explained to Stanton, "By going now [the released prisoners] may still raise something for their subsistence for the coming year and prevent suffering next winter." The secretary of war likely did not care if former Confederates suffered, but he did not have the final say. The new president, Andrew Johnson, favored Grant's approach. On June 6 he ordered that the prisoners be released as quickly as rolls could be prepared. On July 20 he called for the immediate release of all remaining Confederate prisoners. The only exceptions were those captured with Jefferson Davis and "any others where special reasons are known to exist for holding them."[22]

Impatient to start south, the Confederate prisoners clearly preferred the president's approach to the question of release. "This is a glorious day, bright & pleasant," Joyes wrote on May 22, "but my desire to get home makes it seem long indeed." According to Mills, the men's enthusiasm to depart tended to slow the process. He explained, "When the officer would call any name, as A. B. Jones, every Jones . . . sometimes as many as forty, would answer and rush for the gate. The sentinel would stop them, and much time would be lost in finding A. B. Jones." He understood their eagerness, however. "The Vicksburg and Gettysburg men were released first," he recalled. "They had been in prison two years, and so anxious were they to get out, that they seemed to forget everything else."[23]

For William G. B. Morris of the 64th North Carolina Infantry, the day of release came on June 12. "Oh what a happy day to be at liberty once more," he wrote. The road ahead, however, would prove to be long. The next day he went by train from Sandusky to Bellaire, Ohio, by way of Newark. There he crossed the Ohio River to Benwood, West Virginia, but was unable to secure passage on an eastbound train. After spending the night at the depot, he caught an early morning train. The engine broke down in mountain country, and Morris made it only to Piedmont, West Virginia. The next day, June 15, the train arrived in Baltimore. From there Morris boarded a Chesapeake Bay steamer on June 16, arriving at Fortress Monroe the following afternoon.

Once again, Morris had to await transportation. On the 19th he was fortunate, catching a train for Petersburg and another for Danville, where he arrived at 9:00 P.M. He reached Charlotte on the 21st. From there it was a four-day walk to his home. Four days after arriving, Morris wrote, "How happy I am to be at home sweet home with my kind friends once more. Bless the Lord he has brought me safe home again."[24]

For Colonel Hill the process of release posed a major administrative challenge. Several prisoners who had not applied to take the oath before Richmond fell claimed that they had made previous applications through friends. On May 13 Hill posted a notice informing them that they must provide proof of their claims. On June 12 he addressed the concerns of the obviously impatient captives:

> From 3 P.M. of the [10th] until 5 P.M. to day I devoted every available moment with the requisite force to the steps necessary to the discharging of Prisoners, intending to dispose of as many cases as practicable. And I gave my personal attention to all of the required measures with a view not only to expedite the work, but to know with what dispatch final settlement with discharge and transportation papers could be made. During the period named 219 cases were disposed of. I was in hopes that I could regularly dispose of 200 cases every day, but there is so much of detail under existing Regulations as to make it practically impossible to average 200 discharged each day. Still there shall be no want of effort to dispatch cases.[25]

Hill was apparently true to his word. On July 5 Hoffman informed Grant that only 150 Confederate officers remained at Johnson's Island. Hill was also preparing to depart. On July 3 Maj. Samuel P. Lee was ordered to assume command of the post as soon as Hill was mustered out of the service. On September 1 Hoffman ordered Lee to transfer one of the remaining 7 prisoners to Fort Delaware and send the other 6 to Fort Lafayette. Among them was Capt. Charles H. Cole, arrested as part of the September 1864 conspiracy. By October 31 only 4 prisoners remained in Union hands. All were political prisoners, and all were incarcerated at Fort Lafayette. The last was freed in March.[26]

Over the next several months the *Register* announced a number of auctions of government property. At the last one, held in April 1866, L. B. Johnson purchased most of the government buildings on his island. Two months later, on June 8, the post was ordered abandoned, the men on duty ordered to Columbus. Like so many men who served there, Johnson's Island had been mustered out of the service.[27]

Notes

ADAH	Alabama Department of Archives and History, Montgomery
Duke	Rare Book, Manuscript, and Special Collections Library, Duke Univ., Durham, N.C.
Filson	Filson Historical Society, Louisville, Ky.
LC	Library of Congress, Washington, D.C.
MDAH	Mississippi Department of Archives and History, Jackson
NA	National Archives and Records Administration, Washington, D.C.
OCGPLTS	Office of the Commissary General of Prisoners, Letters and Telegrams Sent, Record Group 249, National Archives
OR	*The War of the Rebellion: A Compilation of the Official Records of the Union and Confederate Armies,* 128 vols. (Washington, D.C.: 1880–1901). Unless otherwise noted all references will be to Series II. Citations will be to volume and page number(s).
RG	Record Group
SHC, UNC	Southern Historical Collection, Univ. of North Carolina Library, Chapel Hill
USAMHI	United States Army Military History Institute, Carlisle Barracks, Pa.
UVA	Univ. of Virginia Library, Charlottesville
WHMC	Western Historical Manuscript Collection, Univ. of Missouri, Columbia

1. *"Decidedly the Best Location"*

1. Patricia L. Faust (ed.), *Historical Times Illustrated Encyclopedia of the Civil War* (New York: Harper & Row, 1986), 485.

2. *OR,* 3: 8.

3. Leslie Gene Hunter, "Warden for the Union: General William Hoffman (1807–1884)," Ph.D. dissertation, Univ. Arizona, 1971, 2–15, 23–26, 30–32; Charles

W. Sanders Jr., *While in the Hands of the Enemy: Military Prisons of the Civil War* (Baton Rouge: Louisiana State Univ. Press, 2005), 68.

4. *OR,* 3: 54–56.

5. Ibid., 56–58.

6. Ibid., 122–23, 135–36.

7. *Sandusky Register,* Dec. 7, 1861, Aug. 20, 1891.

8. Ibid.; Hoffman to Meigs, Jan. 27, 1862, OCGPLTS; *OR,* 3: 231.

9. Ibid., 129, 238, 241–42; Hoffman to Col. John Symington, Dec. 28, 1861, OCGPLTS; Hunter, "Warden for the Union," 39.

10. Hoffman to Meigs, Jan. 3, Feb. 5, 1862, OCGPLTS; *OR,* 3: 257; Hunter, "Warden for the Union," 37–38.

11. *Sandusky Register,* Aug. 20, 1891; *OR,* 3: 163, 171.

12. Ibid., 479–80.

13. Hunter, "Warden for the Union," 34–35; *OR,* 3: 590.

14. Ibid., 196, 209, 284.

15. Ibid., 123, 124, 163; Hoffman to Gen. Lorenzo Thomas, Dec. 28, 1861, OCG-PLTS; Hoffman to Gen. C. P. Buckingham, Jan. 7, 1862, OCGPLTS.

16. *Sandusky Register,* Jan. 1, 1862.

17. Ibid., Jan. 21, Mar. 4, 1862.

18. *OR,* 3: 436–37, 505–6.

19. Ibid., 317, 326–27.

20. Ibid., 271–72.

21. Hunter, "Warden for the Union," 40.

2. *"A Prison for Officers Alone"*

1. Hoffman to Meigs, Mar. 2, 13, 1862, OCGPLTS; *OR,* 3: 382.

2. Ibid., 408, 453.

3. *Sandusky Register,* Apr. 11, 1862.

4. *OR,* 3: 448, 465–66.

5. Ibid., 383–384, 405, 6: 759; Charles E. Frohman, *Rebels on Lake Erie* (Columbus: Ohio Historical Society, 1965), 4–5.

6. Entry for Apr. 29, 1862, John Henry Guy Diary, in Mack Curle (ed.), "The Diary of John Henry Guy, Captain, Goochland Light Artillery," *Goochland County Historical Society Magazine,* 33 (2001): 22–23.

7. Entry for May 1, 1862, Andrew Jackson Campbell Diary, in Jill Knight Garrett (ed.), *The Civil War Diary of Andrew Jackson Campbell* (Columbia, Tenn: Printed by author, 1965), 35.

8. Entries for May 19, July 23, 1862, Campbell Diary, in ibid., 36, 43.

9. Hoffman to Commanding Officer, Camp Douglas, June 21, 1862, OCGPLTS; entry for May 28, 1862, William Henry Asbury Speer Diary, in James B. Murphy (ed.), "A Confederate Soldier's View of Johnson's Island," *Ohio History* 79, no. 2 (Spring 1970), 101–2.

10. Entries for June 20–21, 1862, Speer Diary, in ibid., 105–6.

11. Entries for June 20–21, 1862, Edward William Drummond Diary, in Roger S. Durham (ed.), *A Confederate Yankee: The Journal of Edward William Drummond, a Confederate Soldier from Maine* (Knoxville: Univ. of Tennessee Press, 2004), 71–72.

12. Entries for June 21, 24, July 5, 1862, Drummond Diary, in ibid., 73, 74, 81.

13. Entries for Apr. 15, 16, May 14, 1862, Guy Diary, in Curle (ed.), "Diary of Guy," 16–17, 36.

14. Entries for June 30, July 8, 1862, Guy Diary, in ibid., 54–55; entry for June 30, 1862, Speer Diary, in Murphy, "Confederate Soldier's View of Johnson's Island," 108; entries for June 30, July 1, 1862, Drummond Diary, in Durham, *Confederate Yankee,* 78–79; entries for June 30, July 1, 1862, Campbell Diary, in Garrett, *Diary of Campbell,* 40.

15. Entries for July 7, 18, 24, 1862, Drummond Diary, in Durham, *Confederate Yankee,* 85, 88, 90; entry for July 6, 1862, Speer Diary, in Murphy, "Confederate Soldier's View of Johnson's Island," 109; entry for June 2, 1862, Campbell Diary, in Garrett, *Diary of Campbell,* 38.

16. Entry for July 31, 1862, Campbell Diary, in ibid., 44; entry for July 13, 1862, Richard L. Gray Diary, UVA; entry for May 12, 1862, Guy Diary, in Curle, "Diary of Guy," 35; entries for July 2, 5, 1862, Drummond Diary, in Durham, *Confederate Yankee,* 80–81.

17. Entry for July 13, 1862, Gray Diary, UVA; entries for July 18, 28, Aug. 2, 1862, Guy Diary in Curle, "Diary of Guy," 56, 59, 60.

18. Entry for June 24, 1862, Drummond Diary, in Durham, *Confederate Yankee,* 74.

19. Entry for June 22, 1862, Speer Diary, in Murphy, "Confederate Soldier's View of Johnson's Island," 107; entry for July 13, 1862, Gray Diary, UVA; entry for July 28, 1862, Guy Diary, in Curle, "Diary of Guy," 58; entry for July 22, 1862, Campbell Diary, in Garrett, *Diary of Campbell,* 43.

20. Entry for July 28, 1862, Guy Diary, in Curle (ed.), "Diary of Guy," 58; entry for July 13, 1862, Gray Diary, UVA; entry for June 22, 1862, Speer Diary, in Murphy, "Confederate Soldier's View," 107.

21. Entry for June 21, 1862, Speer Diary, in Murphy, "Confederate Soldier's View," 107; entries for May 21, 29, 1862, Campbell Diary, in Garrett, *Diary of Campbell,* 37, 38.

22. Entries for June 14–15, 1862, Campbell Diary, in Garrett, *Diary of Campbell,* 38–39; *Sandusky Register,* June 19, 23, 1862.

23. Entry for Aug. 9, 1862, Campbell Diary, in Garrett, *Diary of Campbell,* 50; entry for Aug. 8, 1862, Speer Diary, in Murphy, "Confederate Soldier's View of Johnson's Island," 110; entry for Aug. 8, 1862, Drummond Diary, in Durham, *Confederate Yankee,* 93–94; entry for Aug. 9, 1862, Gray Diary, UVA.

24. Entry for July 19, 1862, Drummond Diary, in Durham, *Confederate Yankee,* 88–89; entry for July 20, 1862, Campbell Diary, in Garrett, *Diary of Campbell,* 42.

25. *OR,* 4:38, 42.

26. Ibid., 87–89.

27. Ibid., 167–68; Frohman, *Rebels on Lake Erie,* 72.

3. *"Everything in Prison Is Elated"*

1. Eugene Marvin Thomas III, "Prisoner of War Exchange During the American Civil War," Ph.D dissertation, Auburn Univ., 1976, 24–32.

2. *OR,* 3: 51–52, 155, 158, 165, 167, 175–77, 181, 183–84; Sanders, *While in the Hands of the Enemy,* 82–83; Thomas, "Prisoner of War Exchange," 50–51.

3. Sanders, *While in the Hands of the Enemy,* 33–37.

4. *OR,* 3: 157, 183, 211, 254, 301–2, 322.

5. Ibid., 4: 53, 174; Thomas, "Prisoner of War Exchange," 87–90.

6. *OR,* 4: 265–68.

7. Entries for June 24, 28, 29, July 14, 17, 1862, Drummond Diary, in Durham, *Confederate Yankee,* 74, 78, 86, 87.

8. Entry for July 24, 1862, Guy Diary, in Curle, "Diary of Guy," 58; entries for July 24, 25, 1862, Drummond Diary, in Durham, *Confederate Yankee,* 90.

9. Roger Pickenpaugh, *Captives in Gray: The Civil War Prisons of the Union* (Tuscaloosa: Univ. of Alabama Press, 2008), 49–51.

10. Entry for Aug, 10, 1862, Drummond Diary, in Durham, *Confederate Yankee,* 94–95; entry for Aug, 10, 1862, Campbell Diary, in Garrett, *Diary of Campbell,* 51.

11. Entries for July 9, Aug. 10–11, 1862, Drummond Diary, in Durham, *Confederate Yankee,* 83, 94–95; entry for Aug. 27, 1862, Guy Diary, in Curle, "Diary of Guy," 65.

12. *OR,* 4: 435–36.

13. Entry for Aug. 31, 1862, Guy Diary, in Curle, "Diary of Guy," 66; entry for Aug. 31, 1862, Drummond Diary, in Durham, *Confederate Yankee,* 100.

14. *Sandusky Register,* Sept. 2, 1862.

15. Entry for Sept. 5, 1862, Gray Diary, UVA; entry for Sept. 5, 1862, Drummond Diary, in Durham, *Confederate Yankee,* 100–1.

16. Entry for Sept. 5, 1862, Drummond Diary, in Durham, *Confederate Yankee,* 101; entry for Sept. 5, 1862, Gray Diary, UVA.

17. Entry for Sept. 8, 1862, Drummond Diary, in Durham, *Confederate Yankee,* 101; entry for Sept. 9, 1862, Gray Diary, UVA.

18. Walter F. Meier (ed.), "A Confederate Private at Fort Donelson," *American Historical Review* 31, no. 3 (Apr. 1926): 483; entries for Sept. 12, 19, 1862, Gray Diary, UVA.

19. *Sandusky Register,* Sept. 5, 1863; *OR,* 4: 591, 605–6, 629.

20. *OR,* 4: 375, 499–500, 734, 760; Hoffman to Col. Joseph H. Tucker, Sept. 9, 1862, OCGPLTS.

21. *OR,* 8: 987–91.

22. Ibid., 6: 369.

23. Ibid., 5: 556–57; Frohman, *Rebels on Lake Erie,* 58.

24. Frohman, *Rebels on Lake Erie,* 59–62.

25. Entry for Oct. 23, 1863, Robert Bingham Diary, SHC, UNC; entry for Oct. 23, 1863, Joseph Kern Diary, SHC, UNC.

26. *OR,* 5: 691, 702–3.

27. Pickenpaugh, *Captives in Gray,* 65–67.

4. "It Requires Only Proper Energy and Judgment"

1. *OR,* 8: 991–99.

2. Pickenpaugh, *Captives in Gray,* 70–71.

3. Joseph T. Durkin (ed.), *John Dooley, Confederate Soldier, His War Journal* (Washington, D.C.: Georgetown Univ. Press, 1945), 107–11, 124–27.

4. Entries for Aug. 22–24, 1863, Dooley Diary, in ibid., 134–37.

5. Entries for July 2–6, 1864, Edward DeWitt Patterson Journal, in John G. Barrett, *Yankee Rebel: The Civil War Journal of Edmund DeWitt Patterson* (Chapel Hill: Univ. of North Carloina Press, 1966), 117–20.

6. Entries for July 16–20, 1864, Patterson Journal, in ibid., 122–24.

7. Undated entries, ca. July 1863, Thomas Jones Taylor Journal, in Lillian T. Wall and Robert M. McBride, "'Extraordinary Perseverance,' The Journal of Capt. Thomas J. Taylor, C.S.A.," *Tennessee Historical Quarterly,* 31 (1972): 339–40; entries for July 16–22, 1863, J. L. Stockdale Diary, ADAH.

8. Undated entries, ca. July 1863, Taylor Journal, in Wall and McBride, "'Extraordinary Perseverance,'" 340–42; entries for July 26–29, 1863, Stockdale Diary, ADAH.

9. Undated entries, ca. Dec. 1864, Virgil S. Murphy Diary, SHC, UNC.

10. Ibid.

11. Ibid.; entry for May 31, 1864, William Peel Diary, MDAH.

12. Undated entry, ca. Dec. 1864, Murphey Diary, SHC, UNC; undated entry, ca. July 1863, Taylor Journal, in Wall and McBride, "'Extraordinary Perseverence,'" 344–45.

13. Entry for July 21, 1863, Patterson Journal, in Barrett, *Yankee Rebel,* 124; entry for July 22, 1863, Bingham Diary, SHC, UNC.

14. *OR,* 6: 256, 330.

15. Ibid., 364–66.

16. Ibid., 395–96.

17. Ibid., 422–24.

18. Ibid., 433–34.

5. *"This Horrid Life of Inactivity"*

1. Undated entry, ca. Dec. 1864, Murphey Diary, SHC, UNC; entry for June 12, 1864, Patterson Diary, in Barrett, *Yankee Rebel,* 171–72; entry for Jan. 9, 1864, James Mayo Diary, LC.

2. Entry for Aug. 3, 1863, Stockdale Diary, ADAH; Thomas Gibbes Morgan to brother, Dec. 16, 1863, Thomas Gibbes Morgan Papers, Duke; entry for Oct. 23, 1864, John Joyes Diary, Filson.

3. Entries for Nov. 12, Dec. 11, 1863, Mayo Diary, LC; entry for Aug. 3, 1864, Patterson Diary, in Barrett, *Yankee Rebel;* entry for Feb. 10, 1865, Joyes Diary, Filson; *OR,* 8: 258.

4. William G. Woods to cousin, Oct. 26, 1864, William G. Woods Papers, Duke; undated entry, E. John Ellis Diary, in Martina Buck, "A Louisiana Prisoner-of-War on Johnson's Island, 1863–1865," *Louisiana History* 4, no. 3 (Summer 1963): 236.

5. Entry for Nov. 24, 1863, Patterson Diary, in Barrett, *Yankee Rebel,* 145–46; Morgan to mother, Dec. 9, 1863, Morgan Papers, Duke; Merriwether Jeff Thompson, Memoirs, WHMC.

6. Undated entry, Ellis Diary, in Buck, "Louisiana Prisoner-of-War," 236; entries for Sept. 19–20, 1863, Bingham Diary, SHC, UNC.

7. Woods to cousin, Oct. 26, 1864, Woods Papers, Duke; Daniel S. Printup to "Ava," Dec. 3, 1863, Daniel S. Printup Papers, Duke; James A. Riddick to cousin, Feb. 5, 1864, James A. Riddick Papers, Duke.

8. Entry for June 21, 1863, W. B. Gowen Diary, Texas State Library and Archives Commission, Austin; entry for Mar. 7, 1864, Mayo Diary, LC.

9. Entries for Mar. 5, 7, 1864, Peel Diary, MDAH; entry for July 20, 1864, Patterson Diary, in Barrett, *Yankee Rebel,* 181.

10. Entries for Mar. 5, 6, June 26, 1864, Peel Diary, MDAH; entry for Mar. 4, 1864, Mayo Diary, LC; entry for Mar. 2, 1864, Patterson Journal, in Barrett, *Yankee Rebel,* 158–59.

11. Entry for Dec. 30, 1863, Taylor Diary, in Wall and McBride (eds.), "'Extraordinary Perseverance,'" 351; undated entry, ca. Jan. 1865, Murphey Diary, SHC, UNC.

12. Entry for Aug. 8, 1863, Mayo Diary, LC; entries for Mar. 26, May 5, 1864, Peel Diary, MDAH.

13. Frohman, *Rebels on Lake Erie,* 62–65; entry for Sept. 2, 1864, Peel Diary, MDAH; entry for Sept. 2, 1864, Patterson Diary, in Barrett, *Yankee Rebel,* 191.

14. Entry for Aug. 5, 1863, Stockdale Diary, ADAH; entry for Jan. 7, 1865, Mayo Diary, LC; entry for Nov. 18, 1863, Dooley Journal, in Durkin, *John Dooley,* 148.

15. Entry for Apr. 1, 1864, John Philip Thompson Diary, UVA; entry for Apr. 1, 1864, Peel Diary, MDAH; entry for Apr. 1, 1864, Dooley Journal, in Durkin, *John Dooley,* 159–60.

16. Entry for July 7, 1863, Kern Diary, SHC, UNC; entry for July 7, 1863, Gowen Diary, Texas State Library and Archives Commission, Austin; entry for Oct. 15, 1863, Stockdale Diary, ADAH.

17. Entry for Jan. 22, 1865, Dooley Journal, in Durkin, *John Dooley,* 165; entry for Mar. 15, 1864, Peel Diary, MDAH.

18. Pickenpaugh, *Captives in Gray,* 102–3; entry for Nov. 8, 1864, Peel Diary, MDAH; entry for Nov. 10, 1864, Thompson Diary, UVA.

19. Entry for Aug. 3, 1863, Stockdale Diary, ADAH; entry for Dec. 26, 1864, Joyes Diary, Filson; undated entry, ca. Dec. 1864, Murphey Diary, SHC, UNC.

20. Undated entry, ca. Dec. 1864, Murphey Diary, SHC, UNC; entry for Jan. 8, 1864, John M. Porter Diary, Filson; entry for Mar. 30, 1864, Peel Diary, MDAH; *Confederate Veteran* 3 (1897): 470; entry for Sept. 1, 1863, Stockdale Diary, ADAH.

21. Entries for Sept. 2, 8, 16, 1863, Stockdale Diary, ADAH; entries for Sept. 7, 9, 11, 1863, Mayo Diary, LC.

22. Entry for Feb. 22, 1864, Mayo Diary, LC; entry for Feb. 22, 1864, Dooley Journal, in Durkin, *John Dooley,* 159; entry for Feb. 22, 1864, Peel Diary, MDAH.

23. Entry for Aug. 29, 1863, Mayo Diary, LC; entry for Sept. 4, 1863, Kern Diary, SHC, UNC; entry for June 23, 1864, Peel Diary, MDAH.

24. Entries for Sept. 22, 26, Nov. 30, Dec. 12, 1863, Dooley Journal, in Durkin, *John Dooley,* 144–45, 146, 152, 153; entry for Nov. 13, 1863, Bingham Diary, SHC, UNC.

25. Entry for Apr. 19, 1864, Peel Diary, MDAH; undated entry, ca. Nov. 1863, Taylor Journal, in Wall and McBride, "'Extraordinary Perseverance,'" 344; entry for July 24, 1863, Bingham Diary, SHC, UNC; entry for Aug. 25, 1863, Patterson Journal, in Barrett, *Yankee Rebel,* 131.

26. Entries for June 18–19, 1864, Peel Diary, MDAH; entry for June 17, 1864, Patterson Journal, in Barrett, *Yankee Rebel,* 172; entries for July 9, 12, 1863, Bingham Diary, SHC, UNC.

27. Entry for July 26, 1864, Dooley Journal, in Durkin, *John Dooley,* 163; entries for July 14, 16, 30, 1864, Thompson Diary, UVA; entries for July 29, 31, 1864, Peel Diary, MDAH.

28. Entry for Aug. 27, 1864, Peel Diary, MDAH; entry for Aug. 27, 1864, Patterson Journal, in Barrett, *Yankee Rebel,* 190.

29. Entry for Jan. 20, 1864, Bingham Diary, SHC, UNC; entries for Jan. 20, 21, 1864, Thompson Diary, UVA; Thompson, Memoirs, WHMC.

6. *"A Matter of Necessity"*

1. Morgan to mother, Dec. 9, 1863, Morgan Papers, Duke; entry for July 30, 1863, Bingham Diary, SHC, UNC.

2. Entry for Aug. 25, 1863, Dooley Journal, in Durkin, *John Dooley,* 138–39; undated entry, ca. Nov. 1864, Taylor Journal, in Wall and McBride, "'Extraordinary Perseverance,'" 343.

3. Entries for Mar. 31, Apr. 1, 1864, Peel Diary, MDAH; entry for Sept. 26, 1863, Bingham Diary, SHC, UNC; Pickenpaugh, *Captives in Gray,* 185.

4. J. G. De Roulhac Hamilton (ed.), *The Papers of Randolph Shotwell,* 2 vols. (Raleigh: North Carolina Historical Commission, 1931), vol. 2, 140–41.

5. Entry for July 30, 1863, Bingham Diary, SHC, UNC.

6. Entry for Feb. 14, 1864, Bingham Diary, SHC, UNC; entry for Feb. 1, 1864, Patterson Journal, in Barrett, *Yankee Rebel,* 157; Frohman, *Rebels on Lake Erie,* 16.

7. Entry for Mar. 8, 1864, Peel Diary, MDAH; entry for Mar. 9, 1864, Mayo Diary, LC.

8. Undated entry, ca. Nov. 1864, Taylor Journal, in Wall and McBride, "'Extraordinary Perseverance,'" 343.

9. Entries for May 17, 18, 1864, Thompson Diary, UVA; entry for Oct. 27, 1863, Dooley Journal, in Durkin, *John Dooley,* 146–47.

10. Entry for Sept. 7, 1864, Peel Diary, MDAH; Luther Rice Mills, Reminiscences, SHC, UNC.

11. Entry for July ?, 1863, Kern Diary, SHC, UNC.

12. Undated entry, ca. Nov. 1864, Taylor Journal, in Wall and McBride, "'Extraordinary Perseverance,'" 344; entry for Dec. 18, 1864, Thompson Diary, UVA; Pickenpaugh, *Captives in Gray,* 114.

13. Michael P. Gray, *The Business of Captivity: Elmira and Its Civil War Prison* (Kent, OH: Kent State Univ, Press, 2001), 78–82.

14. Entries for Feb. 4, 5, 20, Mar. 15, Apr. 12, 15, 18, May 17, 30, June 29, July 1, 1864, Peel Diary, MDAH.

15. Entries for July 7, 18, 20, 1864, in ibid.

16. Entries for July 27, Aug. 25, Nov. 23, 1865, in ibid.

17. Entry for Feb. 2, 1865, Murphey Diary, SHC, UNC; entry for Feb. 21, 1865, Dooley Diary, in Durkin, *John Dooley,* 166–67.

18. *Confederate Veteran* 17 (1909): 28–29.

19. Entry for Feb. 4, 1864, Thompson Diary, UVA.

7. *"A Guard for Unarmed Men"*

1. *OR,* 6: 500; Hoffman to Tod, Nov. 16, 1863, OCGPLTS.

2. Whitelaw Reid, *Ohio in the War: Her Statesmen, Her Generals and Soldiers* (Cincinnati: Moore, Wilstach, and Baldwin, 1868), vol. 2, 654; *OR,* 6: 841.

3. *OR,* 6; 853–54.

4. Ibid., 7: 122–23.

5. Reid, *Ohio in the War,* II, 654; *OR,* 7: 140–41; General Orders 28, Apr. 22, 1864, 34, May 7, 1864, 19, May 8, 1864, Johnson's Island, Ohio, General Orders, RG 393, NA.

6. *OR,* 7: 178.

7. General Orders 29, May 23, 1864, 35, June 1, 1864, 56, June 25, 1864, 64, Aug. 21, 1864, Johnson's Island, Ohio, General Orders, RG 393, NA; Captain and A. A. A. G. to Charles Bates, Oct. 2, 1864, Johnson's Island, Ohio, Letters Sent, RG 393, NA.

8. James F. Crocker, "Prison Reminiscences," *Confederate Veteran,* 14 (1906), 506.

9. Entry for June 8, 1864, Peel Diary, MDAH; entry for June 7, 1864, Patterson Journal, in Barrett, *Yankee Rebel,* 170.

10. Entry for July ?, 1863, Kern Diary, SHC, UNC; entry for Apr. 5, 1864, Peel Diary, MDAH; *Macon Telegraph,* Apr. 26, 1864.

11. General Orders 60, Aug. 5, 1864, 76, Oct. 25, 1864, 82, Dec. 1, 1864, 84, Dec. 6, 1864, Johnson's Island, Ohio, General Orders, RG 393, NA.

12. General Orders 86, Dec. 14, 1864, unnumbered General Orders, Dec. 31, 1864, in ibid.

13. Hill to Commissary of Subsistence, Aug. 22, 1864, Capt. and A. A. A. G. to A. P. & D. Kelley, Dec. 3, 1864, Johnson's Island, Ohio, Letters Sent, RG 393, NA.

14. Hill to E. A. Scovill, Dec. 17, 1864, Johnson's Island, Ohio, Letters Sent, RG 393, NA.

15. Pickenpaugh, *Captives in Gray,* 138–40.

16. Undated entry, ca. July 1863, Taylor Journal, in Wall and McBride, "'Extraordinary Perseverance,'" 346; entry for July 30, 1863, Stockdale Diary, ADAH; entries for Feb. 14, June 27, Sept. 18, 1864, Peel Diary, MDAH.

17. Undated entry, ca. July 1863, Taylor Journal, in Wall and McBride, "'Extraordinary Perseverance,'" 345; entry for July 30, 1863, Stockdale Diary, ADAH.

18. *OR,* 6: 868, 892, 1061, 1073; Col. Ambrose Stevens to Hoffman, Apr. 21, 1864, Camp Morton, Indiana, Letters Sent, Microcopy 598, RG 393, NA.

19. Entry for Jan. 16, 1864, Bingham Diary, SHC, UNC; entry for July 24, 1864, John Washington Inzer Diary in Mattie Lou Teague Crow (ed.), *The Diary of a Confederate Soldier: John Washington Inzer 1834–1928* (Ashville, AL: Printed by author, 1977), 89.

20. Entry for June 29, 1863, Gowen Diary, Texas State Library and Archives Commission, Austin.

21. Entry for July 15, 1864, Patterson Journal, in Barrett, *Yankee Rebel,* 180; entry for July 16, 1864, Peel Diary, MDAH.

22. Entry for July 26, 1864, Patterson Journal, in Barrett, *Yankee Rebel,* 182–83; entry for July 24, 1864, Peel Diary, MDAH.

23. Entry for June 12, 1864, Peel Diary, MDAH; entry for Dec. 13, 1863, Patterson Journal, in Barrett, *Yankee Rebel,* 149.

8. *"Almost a Fixed Impossibility"*

1. *OR,* 8: 986–1003.

2. B. L. Farinholt, "Escape from Johnson's Island," *Confederate Veteran* 5 (1897): 515; undated entry, ca. Dec. 1864, Murphey Diary, SHC, UNC.

3. Entry for June 3, 1864, Patterson Journal, in Barrett, *Yankee Rebel,* 170; entry for Jan. 18, 1865, Peel Diary, MDAH.

4. Entry for May 29, 1864, Patterson Journal, in Barrett, *Yankee Rebel,* 168–69; entry for June 14, 1864, Peel Diary, MDAH.

5. Entry for Oct. 1, 1863, Dooley Journal, in Durkin, *John Dooley,* 145.

6. Entry for Nov. 3, 1863, Gowen Diary, Texas State Library and Archives Commission, Austin; entry for Nov. 3, 1863, Bingham Diary, SHC, UNC.

7. Entries for Jan. 1–26, 1864, Dooley Journal, in Durkin, *John Dooley,* 154–59; entry for Jan. 3, 1864, Stockdale Diary, ADAH; entry for Jan. 2, 1864, Mayo Diary, LC; entry for Jan. 2, 1864, Bingham Diary, SHC, UNC; William H. Knauss, *The Story of Camp Chase* (Columbus, OH: The General's Books, 1990; repr. of 1906 edition), 225–36.

8. Entries for Feb. 20–21, Mar. 24, 1864, Peel Diary, MDAH; entry for Feb. 21, 1864, Mayo Diary, LC.

9. Hill to Hoffman, Aug. 26, 1864, Johnson's Island, Ohio, Letters Sent, RG 393, NA.

10. Entries for Aug. 7–8, 1864, Patterson Journal, in Barrett, *Yankee Rebel,* 186–87; entries for Aug. 7–9, 1864, Peel Diary, MDAH; entry for Aug. 8, 1864, Inzer Diary, in Crow, *Diary of a Confederate Soldier,* 92

11. Entry for Aug. 10, 1864, Peel Diary, MDAH.

12. *OR,* 7: 840.

13. Ibid., 995–96.

14. Entry for Dec. 13, 1864, Peel Diary, MDAH; entry for Dec. 13, 1864, Joyes Diary, Filson; entry for Dec. 13, 1864, John Reece Diary, GDAH; *OR,* 7: 1,241; Pickenpaugh, *Captives in Gray,* 168.

15. Entry for Dec. 13, 1864, Peel Diary, MDAH; entry for Dec. 13, 1864, Reece Diary, GDAH.

16. *OR,* 7: 1,274–75; ibid., 8: 41–43.

17. Entry for Jan. 22, 1865, Murphey Diary, SHC, UNC; entry for Jan. 22, 1865, Peel Diary, MDAH; entries for Jan. 22, 28, 1865, Inzer diary, in Crow, *Diary of a Confederate Soldier,* 122, 123.

18. Kimberly Brownlee, "Charlie Pierce: A Johnson's Island Rebel," *Timeline* 23, no. 3 (July-Sept. 2006): 40–44.

19. Entry for Jan. 16, 1865, Peel Diary, MDAH; entry for Jan. 16, 1865, Joyes Diary, Filson.

20. Frohman, *Rebels on Lake Erie,* 72–74.

21. Ibid., 73; *OR,* Series I, 43: pt. 2, 922.

22. *OR,* Series I, 233–34; ibid., Series II, 7: 901–2.

23. *Ibid.,* Series 11, 7: 903; Frohman, *Rebels on Lake Erie,* 74–80; Craig W. Hildebrand, "Piracy on Lake Erie," *Michigan History* 82, no. 4 (July-Aug. 1998): 105–8.

24. Entry for Sept. 21, 1864, Patterson Journal, in Barrett, *Yankee Rebel,* 195; entry for Sept. 20, 1864, Joyes Diary, Filson; entries for Sept. 20–21, 1864, Peel Diary, MDAH.

9. *"The Wrath of Hunger"*

1. Pickenpaugh, *Captives in Gray,* 180–81.

2. Entry for Aug. 26, 1863, Patterson Journal, in Barrett, *Yankee Rebel,* 131–32.

3. Entry for Aug. 25, 1863, Dooley Diary, in Durkin, *John Dooley,* 138–39; entry for July 30, 1863, Stockdale Diary, ADAH.

4. *OR,* 7: 484, 504, 803, 840.

5. Entry for Feb. 1, 1864, Porter Diary, Filson.

6. Undated entry, ca. Dec., 1864, Murphey Diary, SHC, UNC.

7. *OR,* 6: 446, 485, 486.

8. Ibid., 625, 774, 1,014–15.

9. Ibid., 7: 110–11.

10. Ibid., 113–14, 123–24.

11. Ibid., 150–51, 183–84, 573–74.

12. Entries for June 5, Aug. 12, 1864, Peel Diary, MDAH.

13. Entries for June 10, Aug. 20, 1864, Patterson Diary, in Barrett, *Yankee Rebel,* 171, 188.

14. Undated entry ca. Dec. 1864, Murphey Diary, SHC, UNC.

15. Entry for Dec. 23, 1863, Bingham Diary, SHC, UNC.

16. Entry for Nov. 18, 1864, Stockdale Diary, ADAH; entry for Oct. 22, 1864, Peel Diary, MDAH.

17. Entry for Sept. 8, 1864, Patterson Journal, in Barrett, *Yankee Rebel,* 192; T. B. Jackson, "Hardships at Johnson's Island," *Confederate Veteran* 12 (1901): 165.

18. Entry for Aug. 20, 1864, Patterson Journal, in Barrett, *Yankee Rebel,* 188; entries for Aug. 21–22, 1864, Thompson Diary, UVA.

19. Entries for Mar. 25, 27, June 10, July 26, Sept. 17, 1864, Peel Diary, MDAH; entry for Sept. 4, 1864, Inzer Diary, in Crow, *Diary of a Confederate Soldier,* 98.

20. Entry for Sept. 14, 1864, Dooley Journal, in Durkin, *John Dooley,* 163; entry for Sept. 17, 1864, Patterson Journal, in Barrett, *Yankee Rebel,* 194–95; entry for Nov. 25, 1864, Peel Diary, MDAH.

21. Undated entry, Ellis Diary, in Buck, "Louisiana Prisoner of War on Johnson's Island," 237–28.

22. *OR,* 7: 766, 803–4, 811.

23. Entry for Jan. 8, 1864, Mayo Diary, LC; entry for Jan. 8, 1864, Bingham Diary, SHC, UNC; entry for Jan. 8, 1864, Thompson Diary, UVA.

24. Entry for Jan. 21, 1865, Peel Diary, MDAH; entry for Jan. 21, 1865, Murphey Diary, SHC, UNC.

25. Entry for Jan. 30, 1865, Murphey Diary, SHC, UNC; entries for Jan. 30–31, 1865, Peel Diary, MDAH.

26. Entries for Jan. 31, Feb. 2, 1865, Peel Diary, MDAH; entry for Feb. 1, 1865, Murphey Diary, SHC, UNC.

10. "A Pitiful Scene"

1. Entries for Dec. 5, 1863, Aug. 26, 1864, Patterson Journal, in Barrett, *Yankee Rebel,* 150, 190; entries for Aug. 26–27, 1864, Peel Diary, MDAH.

2. Entry for Sept. 24, 1864, Peel Diary, MDAH; entry for Sept. 24, 1864, Patterson Journal, in Barrett, *Yankee Rebel,* 196–98.

3. Entry for Sept. 24, 1864, Patterson Journal, in Barrett, *Yankee Rebel,* 197–98; entry for Sept. 24, 1864, Peel Diary, MDAH.

4. *OR,* 7: 876–77; entry for Sept. 24, 1864, Peel Diary, MDAH; entry for Sept. 24, 1864, Patterson Journal, in Barrett, *Yankee Rebel,* 198; Isaiah G. W. Steedman to son, June 1, 1891, Isaiah G. W. Steedman Papers, *Civil War Times Illustrated* Collection, USAMHI.

5. Entry for Sept. 24, 1864, Peel Diary, MDAH; entry for Sept. 24, 1864, Patterson Journal, in Barrett, *Yankee Rebel.*

6. Entry for Sept. 26, 1864, Peel Diary, MDAH; W. Gart Johnson, "Prison Life at Harper's Ferry and on Johnson's Island," *Confederate Veteran* 2 (1894): 242.

7. *OR,* 7: 912–13; entries for Sept. 24, 27, 1864, Peel Diary, MDAH; entry for Sept. 26, 1864, Patterson Journal, in Barrett, *Yankee Rebel,* 198–199.

8. Entry for Jan. 25, 1865, Murphey Diary, SHC, UNC; Printup to wife, Jan. 6, 1864, Printup Papers, Duke; entry for May 3, 1864, Porter Diary, Filson.

9. Thomas W. and Jeanne Appelhans Schmidlin, *Thunder in the Heartland: A Chronicle of Outstanding Weather Events in Ohio* (Kent, OH: Kent State Univ. Press, 1996), 86; Pickenpaugh, *Captives in Gray,* 203–4.

10. Entries for Jan. 1–2, 1864, Stockdale Diary, ADAH; entry for Jan. 1, 1864, Bingham Diary, SHC, UNC; entry for Jan. 1, 1864, Mayo Diary, LC; entry for Jan. 1, 1864, Porter Diary, Filson.

11. Entry for Jan. 11, 1864, Stockdale Diary, ADAH; entry for Jan. 14, 1864, Mayo Diary, LC; *OR,* 8: 994–99.

12. Undated entry, ca. Dec. 1864, Murphey Diary, SHC, UNC; entry for Dec. 4, 1863, Bingham Diary, SHC, UNC; entry for Nov. 4, 1864, Joyes Diary, Filson; entries for Oct. 21, Nov. 18, 1863, Jan. 21, 31, Feb. 17, Mar. 13, 1864, Stockdale Diary, ADAH.

13. Entry for Oct. 4, 1863, Dooley Journal, in Durkin, *John Dooley,* 145; entry for Aug. 5, 1863, Stockdale Diary, ADAH.

14. Entry for Dec. 4, 1863, Bingham Diary, SHC, UNC; entry for Dec. 25, 1863, Mayo Diary, LC; Farinholt, "Escape from Johnson's Island," 515.

15. *OR,* 6: 899–902.

16. Hill to Capt. C. P. Horton, June 26, 1864, Johnson's Island, Ohio, Letters Sent, RG 393, NA; *OR,* 7: 484–48, 553–54, 1067; undated entry, ca. Dec. 1864, Murphey Diary, SHC, UNC.

17. *OR,* 6: 826–30.

18. Ibid., 7: 484–86.

19. Ibid., 6: 517–18; ibid., 7: 421, 484, 695, 803.

20. Entry for Feb. 20, 1864, Peel Diary, MDAH; undated entry, ca. Dec. 1864, Murphey Diary, SHC, UNC.

21. Entries for Dec. 22, 23, 1863, Jan. 11, 1864, Bingham Diary, SHC, UNC; entry for Jan. 8, 1864, Taylor Journal, in Wall and McBride, "'Extraordinary Perseverance,'" 352; *Macon Telegraph,* Apr. 26, 1864.

22. Steedman to son, June 1, 1891, Steedman Papers, *Civil War Times Illustrated* Collection, USAMHI.

23. Pickenpaugh, *Captives in Gray,* 208–10; *OR,* 6: 827, 852–54, 7: 485, 504–5; Steedman to son, June 1, 1891, Steedman Papers, *Civil War Times Illustrated* Collection, USAMHI.

24. Entry for Feb. 23, 1865, Reece Diary, GDAH.

25. *OR,* 6: 391; entries for Nov. 1, 22, 1863, Jan. 17, 1864, Stockdale Diary, ADAH.

26. "Captain" to Maj. H. Eversinan, Nov. 27, 1864, "Captain" to Lt. F. V. Follett, Nov. 30, 1864, Johnson's Island, Ohio, Letters Sent, RG 393, NA.

11. "Sad and Glad at the Same Time"

1. *OR,* 7: 607.

2. Sanders, *While in the Hands of the Enemy,* 259–60; *OR,* 7: 793, 907, 910–11.

3. Entries for Sept. 15, 16, 20, Oct. 5, 1864, Peel Diary, MDAH.

4. *OR,* 7: 1,260–61, 8: 107.

5. Ibid., 1,275; ibid., 8: 381; *Delaware* (Ohio) *Gazette,* Jan. 13, 1865.

6. Entry for Dec. 22, 1864, Reece Diary, GDAH; entry for Dec. 22, 1864, Joyes Diary, Filson.

7. *OR,* 7: 1,063, 1,101, 1,122.

8. Ibid., 1,117, 1,131, 1,281, 1,286, 1,295; ibid., 8: 12–15, 27, 67–68, 77, 123; Morgan Allen Powell, "Cotton for the Relief of Confederate Prisoners," *Civil War History* 9, no. 1 (Mar. 1963): 29, 32–33.

9. Entry for Mar. 17, 1865, Joyes Diary, Filson; entry for Mar. 18, 1865, Reece Diary, GDAH.

10. *OR,* 8: 63, 170, 363.

11. Entries for Feb. 6, 13, 14, 16, 18, 20, 24, Mar. 1, 1865, Joyes Diary, Filson.

12. Entries for Jan. 22, Feb. 16, 19, 1865, Dooley Journal, in Durkin, *John Dooley,* 165–66.

13. Entries for Feb. 27–Mar. 1, 1865, Dooley Journal, in ibid., 168–73.

14. Johnson, "Prison Life at Harper's Ferry and Johnson's Island," 243; entry for Apr. 11, 1865, Reece Diary, GDAH; entry for Apr. 10, 1865, Joyes Diary, Filson.

15. *Sandusky Register,* Apr. 10, 12, 1865.

16. Entry for Apr. 15, 1865, Reece Diary, GDAH; *Sandusky Register,* Apr. 17–18, 1865.

17. Entry for Apr. 15, 1865, Joyes Diary, Filson; entry for Apr. 15, 1865, Reece Diary, GDAH; undated entry, ca. Apr. 15, 1865, Ellis Diary, in Buck, "Louisiana Prisoner-of-War," 241.

18. *OR,* 8: 1,001; entries for Apr. 13, 20, 1865, Reece Diary, GDAH; *Sandusky Register,* Apr. 20, 1865.

19. Mills, Reminiscences, SHC, UNC.

20. Entries for Apr. 3, 9, 11, 25, 27, 1865, Samuel Thomas McCullough Diary, LC.

21. Mills, Reminiscences, SHC, UNC; entries for Apr. 29, May 1, 5, 6, 1865, Joyes Diary, Filson; *Sandusky Register,* May 8, 1865.

22. *OR,* 8: 538, 556, 585, 641, 709–10.

23. Entry for May 22, 1865, Joyes Diary, Filson; Mills, Reminiscences, SHC, UNC.

24. Entries for June 12–29, 1865, William G. B. Morris Diary, USAMHI.

25. Hill, Notice to Prisoners of War, May 13, June 12, 1865, Johnson's Island, Ohio, Letters Sent, RG 393, NA.

26. *OR,* 8: 695, 701, 739; Pickenpaugh, *Captives in Gray,* 237.

27. Frohman, *Rebels on Lake Erie,* 69–71.

Bibliography

Manuscripts

Alabama Department of Archives and History, Montgomery
    Stockdale, J. L., Diary
Rare Book, Manuscript, and Special Collections Library, Duke Univ., Durham, N.C.
    Morgan, Thomas Gibbes, Papers
    Printup, Daniel S., Papers
    Riddick, James A., Papers
    Woods, William, G., Papers
Filson Historical Society, Louisville, Ky.
    Joyes, John, Diary
    Porter, John M., Diary
Georgia Department of Archives and History, Morrow
    Reece, John, Diary
Library of Congress, Washington, D.C.
    Mayo, James, Diary
    McCullough, Samuel Thomas, Diary
Mississippi Department of Archives and History, Jackson
    Peel, William, Diary
National Archives and Records Administration, Washington, D.C.
    Johnson's Island, Ohio, General Orders, RG 393
    Johnson's Island, Ohio, Letters Sent, RG 393
    Office of the Commissary General of Prisoners, Letters and Telegrams Sent, RG 249
Texas State Library and Archives Commission, Austin
    Gowen, W. B., Diary
United States Army Military History Institute, Carlisle Barracks, Pa.
    Morris, William G. B., Diary
    Steedman, Isaiah G. W., Letter (*Civil War Times Illustrated* Collection)
Western Historical Manuscript Collection, Univ. of Missouri, Columbia
    Thompson, Merriwether Jeff, Memoirs

Southern Historical Collection, Wilson Library, Univ. of North Carolina, Chapel Hill
    Bingham, Robert, Diary
    Kern, Joseph, Diary
    Mills, Luther Rice, Reminiscences
    Murphey, Virgil S., Diary
Univ. of Virginia Library, Charlottesville
    Gray, Richard L., Diary
    Thompson, John Philip, Diary

Newspapers and Journals

Confederate Veteran
Delaware (Ohio) *Gazette*
Macon (Georgia) *Telegraph*
Sandusky (Ohio) *Register*

Published Primary Sources

Barrett, John G., ed. *Yankee Rebel: The Civil War Journal of Edmund DeWitt Patterson.* Chapel Hill: Univ. of North Carolina Press, 1966.

Buck, Martina, ed. "A Louisiana Prisoner-of-War on Johnson's Island, 1863–1865" *Louisiana History* 4, no. 3 (Summer 1963).

Crow, Mattie Lou Teague, ed. *The Diary of a Confederate Soldier: John Washington Inzer 1834–1928.* Ashville, Ala: Printed by author, 1977.

Curle, Mack, ed. "The Diary of John Henry Guy Captain, Goochland Light Artillery," *Goochland County Historical Society Magazine* 33 (2001).

Durham, Roger S., ed. *A Confederate Yankee: The Journal of Edward William Drummond, a Confederate Soldier from Maine.* Knoxville: Univ. of Tennessee Press, 2004.

Durkin, Joseph T., ed. *John Dooley, Confederate Soldier, His War Journal.* Washington, D.C.: Georgetown Univ. Press, 1945.

Garrett, Jill Knight, ed. *The Civil War Diary of Andrew Jackson Campbell.* Columbia, Tenn.: Printed by author, 1965.

Hamilton, J. G. De Roulhac, ed. *The Papers of Randolph Shotwell.* 2 vols. Raleigh: North Carolina Historical Commission, 1931.

Meier, Walter F., ed. "A Confederate Private at Fort Donelson." *American Historical Review* 31, no. 3 (Apr. 1926).

Murphy, James B., ed. "A Confederate Soldier's View of Johnson's Island." *Ohio History* 79, no. 2 (Spring 1970).

U.S. War Department. *The War of the Rebellion: A Compilation of the Official Records of the Union and Confederate Armies.* 128 vols. Washington, D.C.: Government Printing Office, 1880–1901.

Wall, Lillian T., and Robert M. McBride, eds. "'An Extraordinary Perseverance,' The Journal of Capt. Thomas J. Taylor, C.S.A." *Tennessee Historical Quarterly* 31 (1972).

Secondary Sources

Bissland, James H. *Blood, Tears, and Glory: How Ohioans Won the Civil War.* Wilmington, Ohio: Orange Frazer Press, 2007.

Brownlee, Kimberly. "Charlie Pierce: A Johnson's Island Rebel." *Timeline* 23, no. 3 (July-Sept. 2006).

Downer, Edward T. "Johnson's Island." In William B. Hesseltine, ed., *Civil War Prisons.* Kent, Ohio: Kent State Univ. Press, 1962.

Faust, Patricia L., ed., *Historical Times Illustrated Encyclopedia of the Civil War.* New York: Harper and Row, 1986.

Frohman, Charles E. *Rebels on Lake Erie.* Columbus: Ohio Historical Society, 1965.

Gray, Michael P. *The Business of Captivity: Elmira and Its Civil War Prison.* Kent, Ohio: Kent State Univ. Press, 2001.

Hesseltine, William Best. *Civil War Prisons: A Study in War Psychology.* Columbus: Ohio State Univ. Press, 1998; repr. of 1930 edition.

Hildebrand, Craig W. "Piracy on Lake Erie." *Michigan History* 82, no. 4 (July-Aug. 1998).

Hunter, Leslie Gene. "Warden for the Union: General William Hoffman (1807–1884)." Ph.D. dissertation, Univ. of Arizona, 1971.

Levy, George. *To Die in Chicago: Confederate Prisoners at Camp Douglas, 1862–65.* Gretna, La.: Pelican, 1999.

Knauss, William H. *The Story of Camp Chase.* Columbus, Ohio: The General's Books, 1990; repr. of 1906 edition.

McAdams, Benton. *Rebels at Rock Island: The Story of a Civil War Prison.* Dekalb: Northern Illinois Univ. Press, 2000.

Pickenpaugh, Roger. *Captives in Gray: The Civil War Prisons of the Union.* Tuscaloosa: Univ. of Alabama Press, 2009.

Powell, Morgan Allen. "Cotton for the Relief of Confederate Prisoners." *Civil War History* 9, no. 1 (Mar. 1963).

Reid, Whitelaw. *Ohio in the War: Her Statesmen, Her Generals and Soldiers.* 2 vols. Cincinnati: Moore, Wilstach, and Baldwin, 1868.

Sanders, Charles W., Jr. *While in the Hands of the Enemy: Military Prisons of the Civil War.* Baton Rouge: Louisiana State Univ. Press, 2005.

Schmidlin, Thomas J., and Jeanne Appelhans Schmidlin. *Thunder in the Heartland: A Chronicle of Outstanding Weather Events in Ohio.* Kent, Ohio: Kent State University Press, 1996.

Thomas, Benjamin P., and Harold M. Hyman. *Stanton: The Life and Times of Lincoln's Secretary of War.* New York: Alfred A. Knopf, 1962.

Thomas, Eugene Marvin, III. "Prisoner of War Exchange During the American Civil War." Ph.D. dissertation, Auburn Univ., 1976.

Weigley, Russell F. *Quartermaster General of the Union Army: A Biography of M. C. Meigs.* New York: Columbia Univ. Press, 1959.

Index

Smart Decisions